GOOD FOOD AFLOAT

GOOD FOOD AFLOAT

Tasty and
nutritious recipes
for healthy
shipboard meals.

JOAN BETTERLEY

Gulf Publishing Company
Houston, Texas

This book is dedicated to Rick—
who brought me the joy of sailing.

Good Food Afloat

Copyright © 1986 by International Marine Publishing Company.
Copyright © 1996 by Gulf Publishing Company, Houston, Texas.

Gulf Publishing Company
Book Division
P.O. Box 2608 □ Houston, Texas 77252-2608

10 9 8 7 6 5 4 3 2 1

Library of Congress Cataloging-in-Publication Data
Betterley, Joan.
    Good food afloat : tasty and nutritious recipes for healthy ship-
board meals / Joan Betterley.
        p.   cm.
    Includes index.
    ISBN 0-88415-357-6
    1. Cookery, Marine.   I. Title.
TX840.M7B4923   1996
641.5'753—dc20   95-42381
                                                             CIP

Printed in the United States of America.

CONTENTS

PREFACE

Picture yourself dropping anchor in a favorite secluded cove after a long beat across the bay. You've had a great day of sailing, but now it's getting dark and you're very hungry. Do you fumble in your food locker and treat yourself to another thrilling meal of canned beef stew? With very little extra effort you could be whipping up a delicious but easy chowder made from fresh ingredients.

. . . You've invited friends along for a daysail, and now it's midafternoon and everyone is ready for a snack. You go below and dig out a bag of potato chips and assorted beers and sodas. Have you ever thought what a welcome change it might be to sink your teeth into fresh pineapple chunks and a tangy wedge of cheese?

. . . It's early morning on the tenth day of your cruise and you're waiting for the fog to burn off. With a couple of hours in which to enjoy a leisurely breakfast, you find your thoughts drifting to a nice warm cornbread or pancakes with fresh blueberry sauce. Instead of dreaming, you could be making them. . . .

People are more conscious of proper nutrition today than at any time in the past. Amid mounting scientific evidence of the dangers of too much fat, too much salt, too much sugar, and too little fiber in our diets, we have been learning to wean ourselves away from highly processed foods and to discover the better health and better taste that comes from eating whole grains, lean meats, and fresh vegetables and fruits.

But what happens to this nutritional awareness when we head out to sea? Many sailors seem to feel that healthy cooking and eating are things that must be left ashore. There are obvious reasons, all of them apparently logical: the galley's too small, there isn't room to stow fancy cooking equipment, the food is likely to spill or spoil, and healthy meals take hours to prepare, hours you'd rather spend sailing. Part of the nautical mystique seems to be to grab something quick from a can and save the gracious eating for times in port.

I confess that when I started out as a cruising sailor, I shared many of these same assumptions. Galley cooking looked like a lot of hard work under primitive conditions, and the temptation was strong to avoid it in any way possible. The only problem was that, as a registered dietitian, I found it harder than most people would to ignore the consequences of my "galley anxiety." In reaching for the highly processed foods that (the assumption goes) are more convenient to stow and prepare, I couldn't disregard what I was putting into my body: salt, sugar, saturated fats—that same high-cholesterol, low-food-value diet I spent my time ashore teaching people to avoid. Since my husband and I sailed nearly every weekend between April and October, it was all too easy to calculate that, with about one-third of each week spent on the boat, what we ate during our time afloat became a significant part of our overall nutrition. All that "junk" mounted up!

With this realization before me, I approached galley cooking with a newfound resolve, and to my surprise and relief, I discovered that it was not nearly as difficult as I had feared. It just required common sense and a little practice. Within a few weeks I was turning out fresh, healthy meals and snacks just as I did at home—and you can, too!

Obviously, a ship's galley is not the same thing as a well-stocked kitchen. Your "refrigerator" is likely to be an icebox, much smaller and less cold than its counterpart at home. You can't store as much food for as long a time. Your stove may have only two burners instead of four; if it is fueled by alcohol, it won't cook as fast as your stove at home. You probably won't have a toaster, a blender, a food processor, or a microwave oven (you may not have an oven of any kind). You certainly will not have as much counter space as at home, and what there is either has things on it already (such as sweaters, radio equipment, or charts), or can't have anything left on it because everything has to be stowed before sailing.

But the secret of good food afloat doesn't lie in fancy equipment; it lies in a little advance planning. There is nothing particularly complicated about good nutrition. It is a matter of simple foods put together in simple but tasty combinations. The trick lies in knowing what foods to bring aboard, where to store them, when to use them, and how to put them together in recipes specifically tailored to galley cooking. That is what this book is all about. With a little patience and practice, healthy eating can become as automatic and natural a part of your sailing technique as, say, plotting a course or stowing sails and lines carefully.

You *can* eat good food afloat. This book will show you how.

RECIPES KEY

The recipes in this cookbook use the following symbols for ease in planning:

— *requires a burner*

— *requires an oven*

— *requires a pressure cooker*

— *requires no cooking*

Cooking terms used in this book

Nonstick-sprayed — *lightly coated with a nonstick vegetable oil spray*

Oiled — *lightly coated in polyunsaturated vegetable oil, or lightly greased with corn oil margarine*

1

WHAT IS "GOOD FOOD"?

You probably first heard of the basic four food groups back in elementary school. It may seem old hat, but it's a tried and true method of ensuring an adequate diet, and the starting point for all nutritional planning. To summarize briefly, here are the four groups:

MILK GROUP (for calcium, protein, and vitamins) —
   milk, cheese, yogurt
MEAT GROUP (for protein, iron, vitamins, and minerals) —
   meat, fish, poultry, nuts, eggs, dried beans or peas
FRUITS AND VEGETABLES (for vitamins and fiber)
GRAINS (for carbohydrates, vitamins, minerals, and fiber) —
   bread, cereals, rice, pasta

Aboard ship as well as on land, the first rule of good nutrition is to get a balanced diet with an adequate representation from each of these four groups. An afternoon of junk food won't kill anyone. But on a cruise, even a few days of dietary imbalance (say, no fruits or vegetables) can begin to show up in a logy, "out of sorts" feeling that definitely puts a damper on the fun.

Foods not in the four basic food groups (such as fats, sweets, condiments, and beverages other than milk, water, or juices) don't contribute to nutrition and should be used sparingly. While it's true that a candy bar can deliver a quick lift when your energy is down—such as on a long beat home in a choppy sea—there are other, more nutritious foods that can do the job just as well—and the lift will last longer.

The second basic rule of good nutrition is this: the fresher the food, the better. Here is where sailors are likely to get into trouble. It's easy enough to go to the market and buy a can of fruit cocktail, a bag of potato chips, an instant macaroni and cheese dinner, and a loaf of white bread. This meal may seem balanced at first glance, but a closer look reveals that its quality leaves a good deal to be desired.

The whole idea behind processing food is to make it keep. Basically, this is done by *taking out* elements that are most likely to perish and by *adding in* chemical preservatives to retard spoilage and provide flavor and color. The results may look like food and taste like food (some people would dispute this), but nutritionally speaking, some of these foods bear about the same relationship to full food value as a storm jib bears to a genoa.

For example, when fruits and vegetables are canned, the high temperatures involved in the canning process destroy some of the water-soluble vitamins, and some of the B and C vitamins leach out into the water in the can and are lost. Commercial grains are routinely pounded and bleached, leaving valuable nutrients and fiber behind in the husks. Foods such as potato chips and doughnuts are bathed in fat during the cooking process, and some foods—such as salami and the ever-popular hot dog—are mostly fat to begin with. Unless their labels specifically state otherwise, canned foods are almost inevitably highly salted, subjecting the unsuspecting sailor to substantial increases in his or her sodium intake.

What all this adds up to—as a generation of nutritionally minded people have learned—is that healthful cooking means avoiding those highly processed "convenience" foods and going back to basics; starting with nutritionally sound ingredients and assembling your own finished products. In this way, you can control what goes into your food and use the best possible ingredients for your health. While shopping, try pretending that the food choices available to you are the ones your grandmother had, and forget the rest. Instead of buying bread automatically, consider thinking in terms of whole grain flour, salt, yeast, and water. Instead of processed peanut butter or sugar-saturated canned fruits, try starting with the real McCoys. Healthful cooking is a matter of keeping on hand some basic staples—such as flour, rice, nuts, dried beans and fruits, pasta, spices—and combining them with perishables—fresh fruits and vegetables, lean meats, eggs, cheese—to create meals that are always fresh and new. Nutrition is a relatively new field, and there may be essential nutrients that are still unknown to us. Highly processed and subsequently fortified foods (such as refined breads) give you only the nutrients of which we are aware. Who knows what's missing? If you buy bread, look for a brand that lists *whole* wheat, rye, oat, or corn flour as the first ingredient. "Wheat" flour (without the word "whole" preceding it) means white flour. Some breads are dark in color and appear to be whole grain when they are actually white breads with caramel coloring. *Whole* grains contain fiber and many more nutrients than white flour products.

GETTING STARTED IN THE GALLEY

Ashore, nutritional cooking presents no real logistical problems. Most kitchens have counter and shelf space sufficient for storing canisters of flour, rice, and other staples. Our refrigerators at home are large and cold, and nearby markets (or our own gardens) assure us a continuing supply of fresh produce. When it comes to cruising, it's a different story! The major attractions of processed, prepackaged foods are that they can be stowed almost anywhere, will last almost indefinitely, and, when needed, can be heated easily. Healthy cooking afloat requires some attention to all of these steps. Let's start by imagining ourselves in the galley and considering some of the challenges involved.

Keeping Things Cold

Part of what makes fresh food fresh is that, not having been embalmed in salt, sugar, or preservatives, it still has the capacity to spoil and rot. Much of it needs to stay cold. Obviously, not everything that you routinely cram into your refrigerator at home is going to fit into the icebox on a typical boat. The trick is to learn what things really *have* to be refrigerated and to develop alternative strategies for items that are less sensitive. Here are some general suggestions; specific details will be found in the Menu Planner section at the end of this chapter.

• Plan to use the *real* perishables early in the cruise. Fresh meats and milk, and delicate vegetables and fruits such as spinach, berries, and peaches must be eaten quickly. Plan your menus so that these items are featured first; later you can switch to less perishable foods. For a one-week vacation cruise I usually pack several fresh produce items such as cantaloupes, berries, tomatoes, broccoli, lettuce, cucumbers, and green peppers. I use these in my lunch and dinner menus for the first four or five days. For the last few days of the cruise I rely more on canned foods: for example, I might plan on making Three Bean and Cheese Salad (page 52) and Lemony Tuna and Beans (page 53) for lunches and Baked Ziti with Three Cheeses (page 112) and Instant Fettucine (page 110) for dinners. These recipes contain ingredients that will keep for a long time on a boat and are good alternatives to canned dinners such as beef stew or canned spaghetti.

Incidentally, you can significantly prolong the life of your ice by using a "Cold Blanket" (available from Mainstay Designs, Inc., 42 Margaret Ct., North Suite C95, Toms River, NJ 08753). You simply load your icebox as usual, then lay the blanket over the contents. The cold is trapped next to the food and beverages, and energy isn't wasted cooling empty space. I use it every time we cruise and have found that it doubles the time ice lasts. The "Cold Blanket" costs $10.95 for boats under 30 feet and $13.95 for boats over 30 feet. I think it's well worth the price in convenience alone, since I hate to have to hunt for ice every few days.

• Keep in mind that many things we normally refrigerate at home don't really have to be refrigerated. Eggs will last for three weeks without refrigeration if you turn them every few days to keep the yolks from settling. Cheese can be preserved in oil (see page 7) if you have no ice. Apples, bananas, citrus fruits, and melons last well when stored in a cool, dark place, and potatoes, onions, and some vegetables will keep for two months or more.

• Remember also that many foods normally considered perishable are also available in nonperishable versions. Nonfat dry milk is a thoroughly serviceable substitute for fresh milk; it works well in recipes and can also be used to make fresh yogurt. Beans are nutritionally excellent substitutes for meat, and they last indefinitely.

Storing Things

Stowage of food aboard a vessel is an art, and requires study and practice. On those calm days in port it is all too easy to forget that foods can get knocked about and turned upside down when you sail. Things that can spill must be in secure, lidded containers, and chocked so that they won't fall over. Foods that are brittle or bruise easily, such as eggs and some fruits, need sturdy containers or some sort of swathing.

Many items like eggs and vegetables that you keep in the refrigerator at home can be stored elsewhere on your boat, and probably will be, to conserve valuable icebox space for those items that must be kept cold. Exactly where this "elsewhere" is depends on the size and construction of your boat, the duration of your cruise, and your own ingenuity. Some fruits and vegetables need to be kept in cool, dark places; a locker near the waterline is ideal if it doesn't leak. Others do best in a well-ventilated spot such as a wire mesh hanging basket (if you can afford the space) or a net storage hammock. I have had good success storing fresh produce in a basket sitting casually atop a dropleaf table. The fiddles on the table keep the basket in place under sail, and the sides of the basket confine the produce. Grains and pasta stored in containers of plastic or glass (for specifics, see page 13 in the Menu Planner) can be wedged into whatever nooks and crannies your cabin space makes available; obviously, items you will be using more frequently should be more accessible. Try to store canned goods in a cool spot, near the waterline and not next to the oven, to prolong their life and keep vitamin losses down.

You also have to remember to stow the garbage can properly before you set sail. I don't know how many times I've left it sitting on the galley floor, only to have it spill its contents as soon as we were underway.

Cooking Things

Having the right stove is a big help. Since most of your cooking will make use of your stovetop burners, it's worth noting that some fuels are better than others. My husband and I now have a propane stove, which works well, has a hot flame, and is simple to operate. On an earlier boat we had an alcohol stove that flared alarmingly and boiled water all too slowly. It may seem extravagant to replace a stove that works, but the savings in time and temper can be well worth it.

An oven is very handy for baking potatoes or casseroles and for keeping pancakes warm when making a large batch for a crowd. But if you don't have an oven, you'll find plenty of recipes in this book that don't require one—even for baked goods such as Skillet Poppy Seed Cake (page 141) and Molasses Cakes (page 156).

A pressure cooker is especially useful if you don't have an oven, and it saves cooking time, too. Although I don't use my pressure cooker on a regular basis, I find that foods cooked in it have a wonderful flavor. Pressure cooking also retains vitamins in foods better than any other cooking method. You might want to try Pressure Cooked Hamburger and Potato Dinner (page 91) or Lentil Soup (page 62) to get started if you haven't used a pressure cooker before.

I don't have a hibachi aboard but have included a few recipes for those of you who do. Sailors who cruise in warm climates enjoy the hibachi because it does not add heat to the cabin. While chartering in the Caribbean, my husband and I had our first opportunity to use one. It was a pleasure to watch the coals glow in the dark while we dined in the cockpit, enjoying the feel of balmy breezes on our shoulders.

THE SEAGOING MENU PLANNER

The next several pages offer suggestions on healthy foods to take cruising and how to store and preserve them. The items listed provide the basic ingredients from which the recipes in the following chapters are assembled. The foods are arranged according to the basic four food groups. Both perishable and nonperishable sources are listed. Sometimes, when these basic foodstuffs are themselves in need of simple recipes to put them together (as with nonfat dry milk, page 6, and yogurt, page 7), those recipes appear here.

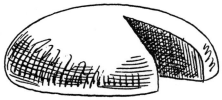

MILK GROUP
Provides calcium, protein, and riboflavin.
Adults need two servings daily.

Perishable Sources
(keep well chilled in icebox)

> **Fresh milk** *(one serving equals 8 ounces)*
> **Yogurt** *(one serving equals 8 ounces)*
> **Cheese** *(one serving equals 1½ ounces)*
> **Cottage cheese** *(one serving equals 16 ounces)*
> **Tofu** *(one serving equals 8 ounces)*
> **Fresh oysters** *(one serving equals 21–27 individual oysters)*
> **Fresh salmon** *(one serving equals 6 ounces)*

Nonperishable Sources

Nonfat dry milk—I like to buy it in envelopes rather than in bulk because it stays fresher longer; store envelopes in a sealed plastic bag and keep a supply on your boat for use in recipes.

To mix, use a lidded jar and shake together ⅓ c. nonfat dry milk powder with slightly less than 1 c. water. To make delicious dry milk beverages, see p. 160.

Hot cocoa mixes *(one serving equals 8 ounces or 1 envelope; see page 160 for a homemade cocoa mix)*

Sterilized milk—If you don't like nonfat dry milk, you might want to try a nonperishable sterilized milk. I tried this while chartering in the British Virgin Islands and found that it tasted exactly like fresh milk. The milk is heated to an ultrahigh temperature for just a few seconds to kill bacteria normally found in milk without destroying valuable vitamins and minerals. Still in a sterile condition, it is then piped into aseptic packaging material. It is available in whole and chocolate in the 8-ounce size and whole and lowfat in the quart size. It will stay fresh for up to 8 months, unopened, without refrigeration. Once opened, it must be refrigerated. One such product, Real Fresh Milk, may be ordered by writing to Real Fresh Milk, Inc., P.O. Box 1551, Visalia, CA 93277.

Yogurt—You can make your own yogurt with nonfat dry milk and either fresh yogurt or freeze-dried yogurt starter (available in health food stores and some dairies). Here are two methods for making yogurt:

- *Thermos Method:*
Boil 3¾ c. water and mix in 1 envelope (or 1⅓ c.) nonfat dry milk to reconstitute. Heat milk to 180 degrees and then let cool to 110 degrees. (It works best if you have a thermometer, but if you don't, heat milk to boiling and let it cool until it feels like bath water; it can't be too hot or it will destroy the yogurt culture.) Dissolve 1 packet of the freeze-dried yogurt starter or 2 Tbsp. of fresh yogurt into a small amount of the lukewarm milk in a cup, then pour it back into the quart of milk. Mix well. Let the milk sit in the thermos for 4 to 8 hours. The longer it sits, the tarter it becomes. Chill or use as is.

- *Oven Method:*
Preheat oven to 275 degrees. Follow above directions and pour milk-yogurt mixture into a covered, clean casserole dish. Turn off oven and place yogurt casserole in oven. Let sit, undisturbed, for 4 to 8 hours; then chill if you have ice. If not, eat as is or use in recipes.

Evaporated skim milk—Use full-strength in place of cream in chowders, sauces, and desserts. (*one serving equals 4 ounces*)

Cheese—Preserve in oil if you have no ice. Buy a fresh round of cheese covered with wax (to be sure that it has not been contaminated or exposed to air.) Cut into chunks—each one the size of a week's supply—and store in separate containers. Completely cover the cheese with safflower, sunflower, or corn oil. The cheese will keep for six months, and the cheese-flavored oil may be used for cooking.

Cottage cheese—Make it with nonfat dry milk: Mix 1 envelope (or 1⅓ c.) nonfat dry milk with 3¾ c. water and let it sit until it curdles. Heat gently to solidify the curds, and strain the liquid (whey). Season with a little salt or herbs if desired.

Canned sardines and salmon (*one serving equals 3 ounces of the former or 6 ounces of the latter*)

MEAT GROUP
Provides protein, iron, niacin, thiamine, and zinc.
Adults need two servings daily.

Perishable Sources
(keep well chilled in icebox)

Fresh meat, fish, shellfish, or poultry—Store in leakproof container close to ice. It's a good idea to choose lean selections and eat them in small portions to avoid getting too much fat, saturated fat, and cholesterol. *(one serving equals 2 ounces cooked)*

Eggs—For weekend cruising I store them in a plastic egg crate made for backpackers and place them on the icebox shelf. For longer cruises, follow instructions below. *(one serving equals 2 eggs)*

Tofu *(one serving equals 8 ounces)*

Nonperishable Sources

Canned lean meat, fish, shellfish, or poultry—Try to store close to the waterline.

Eggs—Although eggs are not really nonperishable, you can make them last a long time. Buy them as fresh as possible and turn them every few days to prevent the yolks from settling. In this manner they will last for three weeks without refrigeration. They will last about three months if you cover them with petroleum jelly and turn them frequently. If immersed in sodium silicate or "waterglass" (once available in any drugstore but now more difficult to find) and turned frequently, they will last for up to six months.

Dried beans and peas—For the sailor on an extended cruise these are excellent substitutes for animal foods (see pages 94–96 for information on protein complementation). Store in glass jars or plastic containers with five bay leaves per one-gallon jar to keep the bugs at bay. *(one serving equals 1 cup)*

Peanut butter—For short cruises, I buy freshly ground peanut butter with no preservatives added. This lasts one to two months without refrigeration. For extended cruises, I buy the "natural" peanut butter with the oil on top and no hydrogenated fats added. Unopened, this should last for many months. *(one serving equals 4 tablespoons)*

Nuts—Buy them unshelled to help prevent rancidity on an extended cruise. Store in jars or plastic containers in a cool, dry spot. *(one serving equals ½–¾ cup, shelled)*

Seeds—Store the same way as nuts. *(one serving equals ½–¾ cup)*

Precooked meals in soft pouches and freeze-dried meals

FRUIT-VEGETABLE GROUP
Provides vitamins A and C and fiber.
Adults need four servings daily
including one serving of a high vitamin C source.
*(One serving of any fruit or vegetable comprises 1 cup of the raw produce
or ½ cup of a cooked, canned, or juice product.)*

Perishable Sources
(store in icebox and use quickly)

Berries
Peaches
Spinach
Romaine lettuce
Very ripe fruits and vegetables
Frozen fruits and vegetables—Store in leakproof containers down on the ice. If they should thaw, try to use them within one day.

Less Perishable Sources

If you're planning a long offshore cruise, you *can* take along fresh fruits and vegetables if you know how to store them properly. The fruits and vegetables listed below will last for a good length of time if you buy and store according to the suggestions given. Keep in mind that your produce will last for much longer if you spend a few minutes daily checking for spoilage spots and turning it.

Fruits

Apples—Green apples last longest, red next, and yellow third. Buy small apples without any bruises; wrap each one in tissue paper and store tightly packed in a dark place; check weekly, cut off bruised spots, and rub spots with lemon juice (use these first).

Bananas—Buy small hands of large, dark green, hard, thick-skinned bananas; store in a dark, cool place. Will last about two weeks.

Citrus fruit (oranges, lemons, limes, and grapefruit)—Buy thick-skinned varieties to reduce risk of bruising; wrap in aluminum foil and store in a cool, dry place. They should keep for at least one month. For a small quantity of lemon or lime juice, puncture the skin with an ice pick, squeeze, and rewrap. Freshen dried out fruit by soaking overnight in lukewarm water or placing in boiling water for five minutes.

Melons—Store in a cool spot; will last six to ten days. Melons are ripe when the stem end is soft, a melon fragrance can be smelled, and seeds, when the fruit is shaken, can be heard sloshing inside.

Pineapple—Will keep for two weeks if purchased green and allowed to ripen. Once ripe, it spoils quickly.

Tangerines—If possible, buy them with their leaves left on. Keep cool and dark in a well-ventilated spot. Check for spoiled ones every few days. Will last up to one month.

Watermelons—Buy small ones and wrap in newspaper; store in a well-ventilated area. Will last three weeks if you buy them unripened.

Vegetables

Avocados—Buy in different stages of ripeness; wrap each one in tissue paper and store in a crate with the greenest ones on the bottom. May keep up to three weeks.

Cabbage—Buy as fresh as possible with the outer leaves intact. Store in a cool, dry place with newspaper between cabbages. Check every few days and remove rotting leaves. Will keep up to one month.

Carrots—Buy large carrots; remove from plastic bags; store in a dry, well-ventilated spot. Check every few days and remove black spots. Will stay crisp up to two weeks in northern climates, one week in the tropics.

Cucumbers—Buy very dark green ones and store out of direct sunlight. Turn every four days. Use as soon as they soften. Will last up to two weeks. Preserve excess cucumbers in a marinade of ½ vinegar and ½ oil.

Green peppers—Wrap in waxed paper and store in a cool spot. Will last up to twenty days in cooler climates and eight to ten days in the tropics.

Lettuce—Buy tightly packed heads with the outside leaves intact. Hang away from direct sunlight, in string bags or wire mesh baskets so that air can circulate. Will keep for up to ten days.

Onions—Buy hard onions without sprouts. Store in a dry, dark place; check weekly. Sprouts are edible. Will last at least two months.

Potatoes—Buy round potatoes with no evidence of eyes or signs of green tinge. Keep completely dry in a well-ventilated, dark place. Inspect once a week and remove sprouts, but don't eat them—they are poisonous! Don't store potatoes with onions because the gases from one deteriorate the other. Will last about two months.

Tomatoes—Buy small ones in different stages of ripeness. Store in cardboard egg boxes. Will last about three weeks.

Turnips—Keep in a cool, dry place. Will last about one month.

Winter squash—Buy small squashes so that they can be used up in one meal. Store in a cool, well-ventilated spot. Will keep for up to seven weeks.

Sweet potatoes and yams—Buy hard, regular-shaped ones. Keep completely dry and store in a well-ventilated, dark spot. Inspect weekly; will last for two months.

Nonperishable Sources

Canned fruits and fruit juices
Dried fruits
Freeze-dried fruits
Canned vegetables and vegetable juices
Dried vegetables
Freeze-dried vegetables
Seeds, grains, and beans for sprouting
(see pages 48–49 for sprouting procedures)

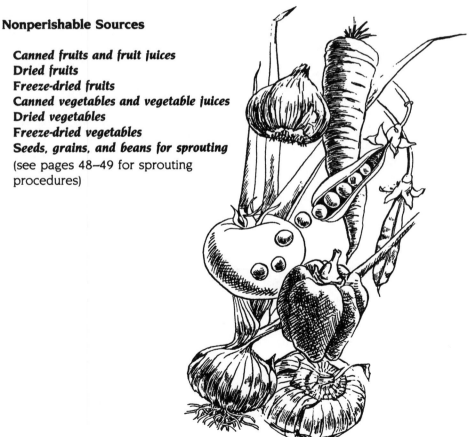

GRAIN GROUP
Provides carbohydrates, thiamine,
niacin, iron, and fiber.
Eat whole grains to get plenty of fiber.
Adults need four servings daily.
(One serving equals one slice of bread.
1 cup of ready-to-eat cereal, or ½ cup cooked cereal, pasta, or grits.)

Perishable Sources

Bread—For a weekend or short cruise, I store bread either on the shelf in the icebox or in a Tupperware bread container. For an extended cruise, you can buy one or two loaves of double-baked bread (bakeries may do this on request); the hard crust keeps mold from forming. Another way to preserve bread is to paint a light coating of vinegar all over it with a pastry brush. This prevents mold. Then place the bread in two or three sealed bags or a plastic container. It will keep for up to two weeks in the tropics and longer in cooler climates.

Nonperishable Sources

Brown rice
Whole grains
Flours
Whole grain cereals
Grits
Barley
Millet
Popcorn

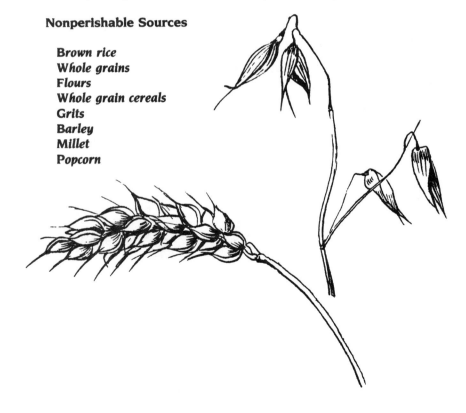

If you are planning an extended cruise, you need to protect the above foods from weevils. I once found a whole locker full of these bugs. They ate right through one plastic or cellophane bag to another. I now try to store all grain-type foods in *glass* jars, because I'm told that these weevils will even eat through plastic containers if very hungry! Here are two methods of protecting your stores from vermin:

- *Bay leaves*—Add five bay leaves per one-gallon container and seal with tape. Replace the leaves every six months. I use this method, and it works.

- *Dry ice*—Although I have not used this method, Shirley Herd Deal, author of *The Cruising Cook*, recommends dropping a 1-inch-diameter lump of dry ice into a one-gallon container (or proportionally smaller amounts if your needs are less). Fill the container with food to within 2 inches of the top. Place the lid on, slightly ajar to allow gas to escape. When all signs of the gas are gone (30 to 60 minutes), tighten the lid as securely as possible and wrap with tape. The weevil larvae should then be dead.

Noodles, spaghetti, pasta, and macaroni—Store in glass or plastic containers. You might want to try these foods in whole wheat form (available in health food stores and some grocery stores) to maximize your fiber intake.

Dry cereals—Store in plastic containers with airtight lids. I use a Tupperware cereal container.

Crackers—Store in plastic containers with airtight seals. My crackers stored in Tupperware were perfectly fresh after a one-month cruise to and from Bermuda, even though the packages were opened. Unsalted crackers stay fresh longer than salted crackers.

Rusks—A great way to preserve extra fresh bread is to cut a loaf of bread into thick slices, then place the slices on racks or trays in a warm oven until crisp and brown. This removes moisture, thus discouraging mold. Store in an airtight container. Will last for months.

Canned brown bread—This is nonperishable and makes a nice treat at sea.

MISCELLANEOUS FOODS

Mayonnaise or mayonnaise-type salad dressing—I always buy very small jars so that opened jars will be used up before they spoil. Store opened jars on ice if possible. If the ice runs out, a partly used jar will keep for at least several days; the vinegar in the mayonnaise acts as a preservative. Eventually, unrefrigerated mayonnaise will spoil. If it smells or tastes rancid, or if it turns yellow, don't use it. If it has not separated and smells and tastes OK, use it without fear. There is no real difference in the keeping quality of mayonnaise versus mayonnaise-type salad dressings.

Margarine—For short cruises, I pack it into a small, airtight container and store it on the icebox shelf. For an extended cruise, Shirley Herd Deal suggests that you can preserve butter or margarine by removing it from its package and packing it in glass jars that have been sterilized in boiling water. Pack the margarine to within 1 inch of the top of the jar, pressing out any air bubbles. Fill each jar to the top with salt, place a piece of muslin over the top, and seal with a tight-fitting screw lid.

Yeast—I buy it in individual packages and store in a cool, dry place. Refrigeration is not necessary.

SALTY THOUGHTS FOR SAILORS

Cruising sailors who eat a lot of canned foods may be greatly increasing their sodium intake without realizing it. Did you know that a half-cup of a canned vegetable contains 60 times as much salt as the same serving of a natural fresh vegetable? Canned and dried meats and prepared grain and rice dishes (canned, and boxed mixes) have similar very dramatic increases in salt content.

Most fresh fruits, fresh and unsalted frozen vegetables, fresh and unsalted frozen meats, grains, pasta, legumes, and nuts are naturally low in sodium. If you learn to cook with less salt and use the salt shaker less, you'll achieve the goal of decreasing your sodium intake, even though you may still eat some high-sodium canned goods.

You'll be amazed at how good foods taste without salt when you let their natural flavors emerge. Here are some salt substitutes that do just that:

- Dry mustard—Mix with a little water to make a paste; spread on chicken or fish or use in salad dressings.
- Garlic—Goes well with meat, fish, poultry, salad dressings, and tomato sauces.
- Hot pepper flakes—Use a *small* amount to spice up vegetables, tomato sauces, casseroles, and soups.
- Curry powder—Use in small amounts without too many other spices. Good with meat, fish, poultry, eggs, rice, and vegetable mixtures.
- Chili powder—Good with almost any dish made with tomatoes.
- Horseradish root—Use freshly grated on fish and chicken.
- Sugar—A pinch of sugar added to vegetables while they cook will bring out their flavor.
- Lemon or lime juice—Tastes great on broccoli or other green vegetables, chicken, and fish.
- Port wine—Goes well with chicken dishes.
- Other herbs and spices—Be creative and try your own combinations.
- Vinegar—Good on cooked and raw vegetables.
- Salt substitute recipe
    1 tsp. chili powder
    2 tsp. ground oregano
    2 tsp. black pepper
    1 Tbsp. garlic powder
    2 Tbsp. dry mustard
    6 Tbsp. onion powder
    3 Tbsp. paprika
    3 Tbsp. poultry seasoning

Mix all seasonings together and put in your salt shaker. Use as you would salt.

2

BREAKFAST

Breakfast in our culture is a badly neglected meal, and the tendency is, if anything, more pronounced aboard a boat. Sailors don't know what they're missing.

One night, my husband Rick and I stopped off at Point Judith Harbor of Refuge while on our way to Block Island. The next morning, the fog was so thick we couldn't see any of the boats anchored nearby. We could have used our radar and picked our way through the fog, but sailing through fog is not my idea of cruising for pleasure. Instead, we elected to stay at anchor and spend the morning reading. To me, fog-forced leisure can be a welcome part of a vacation cruise. Since we had plenty of time, I decided to cook some Banana Bran Pancakes (page 30), which we greatly enjoyed before curling up in our bunks with our favorite books.

If we had waked to clear skies and favorable winds and had wanted an early start, we might have had a cockpit meal of Cornbread (page 32) that I made a day earlier, peanut butter, and orange juice.

One sunny Sunday morning we were in Newport Harbor with two visiting couples aboard. All we had planned was a short, leisurely sail back to Wickford, Rhode Island, later in the day, so I had plenty of time to cook up one of my favorite "company" recipes—Artichoke-Cheese-Scramble (page 41) with Whole Wheat and Raisin Griddle Scones (page 31). We all enjoyed eating at the cockpit table, watching the yachts go by and soaking up the sunshine.

Whether eaten leisurely in the cockpit or while under sail, breakfast is an important meal. You need that fuel to get your body going so that you'll feel better and enjoy your whole day more fully. You can eat more calories daily without gaining weight if you spread them out over three or more meals. The ideal pattern is to eat a large breakfast and lunch and a light evening meal. Most people I've talked to do just the opposite. You may think that you are avoiding calories by skipping breakfast, but probably not. Without breakfast, your body will move more slowly in the morning (to conserve energy), and you will most likely make up for those calories later in meals and snacks. Even if weight control is not a problem for you, several meals a day will keep your blood sugar at its optimum level and make you feel energetic all day long.

VITAMIN C

How many bruises did you get on your last rough voyage? I counted 50 bruises upon arriving in Bermuda after a stormy sail, and realized that I must be more careful about vitamin C the next time. By giving your body's cells the ability to produce collagen, vitamin C makes the walls of the blood vessels firmer and so helps prevent bruising. The first signs of a mild deficiency are easy bruisability and bleeding gums, symptoms noted by many long-distance cruisers.

Large doses of vitamin C taken during a cold may have a small beneficial effect on its severity, but vitamin C cannot reduce the frequency of colds or their duration. High doses in pill form can be harmful to some people. I feel that it's better to get vitamin C naturally, from foods.

An easy way to remember to get your daily dosage is to include it in breakfast food. The accompanying chart suggests how to stow vitamin C on your boat in perishable and nonperishable foods.

Good Sources of Vitamin C

The foods below are listed from highest to lowest in vitamin C content. A quick glance should help you find the foods you need to meet your RDA. Asterisks indicate perishable raw fruits and vegetables that are suitable for storage on an extended cruise, as described on pages 9–11. These fresh foods can supplement nonperishable sources.

RDA = 60 mgms., Adults
　　　 70 mgms., Pregnant Women
　　　 95 mgms., Nursing Women

Perishable Foods

FRUITS	Serving Size	Milligrams Vit. C
Orange juice, fresh	1 c.	124
Strawberries, fresh	1 c.	88
Orange, fresh*	1 medium	80
Grapefruit, fresh*	1 medium	76
Lemon, fresh*	1 medium	53
Lime, fresh*	1 medium	37
Honeydew melon, fresh*	1 piece 2″ deep, 6½″ diameter	35
Cantaloupe, fresh*	¼ of a medium-sized fruit	33
Tangerines, fresh*	2 small	31
Cherries, fresh	20 medium ripe	30

VEGETABLES		
Green pepper, raw*	1 large, whole	128
Broccoli, cooked	1 c.	120
Broccoli, raw	1 stalk, 5½″	113
Brussels sprouts, cooked	6–7	87
Cauliflower, raw	1 c.	78
Greens, cooked	1 c.	60–100
Cauliflower, cooked	1 c.	62
Spinach, raw	3½ oz.	51
Cole slaw	1 c.	47
Cabbage, cooked in small amount of water*	1 c.	46
Tomato, raw*	1 large	46
Sweet potato, baked*	1 large	40
White potato, baked*	1 large	30

Nonperishable Foods
(Store near waterline)

FRUITS		
Orange juice, canned	6 oz.	75
Grapefruit juice, canned	6 oz.	55
Grapefruit segments, canned	½ c.	30

VEGETABLES		
Turnip greens, canned	1 c.	38
Tomatoes, canned	1 c.	34
Tomato juice, canned	6 oz.	29
Spinach, canned	1 c.	26

FIBER AFLOAT

The typical American diet is low in fiber, and the sailor's diet, with its heavy reliance on processed or convenience foods, may be especially so. Breakfast is a good meal in which to boost fiber intake, because you can use whole grain flours in breads, muffins, and pancakes, and you can choose whole grain cereals. To increase the fiber content of processed or cooked cereals, add 1 to 3 Tbsp. of unprocessed bran before serving. All of the grain recipes in this chapter are high in fiber.

I have included some recipes for oat bran, which lowers cholesterol more effectively than any other fiber. Besides using oat bran in recipes, you can eat it cooked, like oatmeal. It is available in health food stores and some grocery stores.

Dietary fiber can be divided into two categories: *insoluble* and *soluble*. Each possesses distinct health advantages. A diet high in insoluble fiber can help prevent a variety of ills from constipation to cancer of the colon. Soluble fiber forms gels that cause carbohydrates to be absorbed into the bloodstream more slowly, preventing dramatic swings in blood sugar levels. Preliminary research also indicates that soluble fibers lower blood cholesterol levels.

Good Sources of Insoluble Fiber

The foods below are listed from highest to lowest in insoluble fiber content. Asterisks indicate foods that stow easily and keep for a long time. See pages 8–13 for specific storage information.

Unprocessed bran*
100% bran cereal*
Kidney beans*
Parsnips
White beans*
Peas[1]
Blackberries
Pinto beans*
Whole grain bread or cereal*
Rye wafers*
Popcorn*
Rye bread*
Pears[1]
Apples*

Potatoes*
Strawberries
Zucchini
Graham crackers*
Tomatoes[1]
Corn grits*
Brown rice*
Summer squash
Lima beans[1]
Brussels sprouts
String Beans[1]
Oats, whole*
Broccoli
Plums

[1]*easily stored if canned*

Good Sources of Soluble Fiber

The foods below are listed from highest to lowest in soluble fiber content. As in the list above, asterisks indicate foods that stow easily and keep well.

Oat bran*
Apples*
Potatoes*
Peas[1]
Broccoli
Carrots[1]
Tangerines
Plums[1]
Zucchini

Summer squash
Strawberries
Apricots[1]
Dried apricots
Grapefruit[1]
Popcorn*
Rye bread
Onions*

[1]*easily stored if canned*

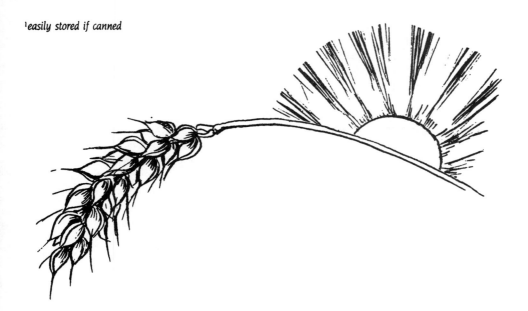

GRAINS FOR BREAKFAST AND OTHER MEALS

Whole grains are a staple on our boat because they're delicious, nutritious, inexpensive, and easily stowed. Rather than the "quick" or "instant" cooking varieties, I like to buy whole or "old-fashioned" grains because they are tastier, chewier, and usually contain more fiber than their refined counterparts.

Store grains in airtight glass jars or plastic containers with bay leaves or fumigated with dry ice (see page 13). If you store them in plastic bags, bugs may hatch and eat right through the bags.

Regular Cooking Method

Use this method to cook the following varieties of grains:

Grain (1 c. dry measure)	Water	Cooking Time
Rolled oats	2 cups	20 minutes
Rolled wheat	2 cups	20 minutes
Rolled rye	2½ cups	10 minutes
Cracked wheat	2 cups	25 minutes
Cracked triticale	4 cups	20 minutes
Coarse cornmeal (polenta)	4 cups	20 minutes
Kasha	2 cups	15 minutes
Bulgur wheat	2 cups	15–20 minutes
Brown rice	2 cups	50 minutes
Millet	3 cups	45 minutes

Bring water, milk, or broth to a boil. If desired, add ¼ to ½ tsp. salt for each cup of grain. Slowly pour in the grain, cook for a minute or two, reduce heat to simmer, and cover and cook for the prescribed time or until all the liquid is absorbed. Use more water if a thinner consistency is desired.

Thermos Method

This method may be used for cooking any of the grains in the chart above. On the evening before you plan to have cooked cereal for breakfast, pour ¾ c. cereal into a pint-size thermos that has been preheated with a rinse of boiling water. Fill to the top with boiling water, and cap. Let stand overnight. By morning, the cereal will be cooked and piping hot. If it's too thick, simply thin with more hot water. This method makes two one-cup servings. I use it often when a long sail is planned and we want to have breakfast while underway.

Pressure Cooker Method

A pressure cooker can be used for the following grains, which would take much longer to cook by the regular stovetop method:

Grain (1 c. dry measure)	Water	Cooking Time
Whole wheat berries	3 cups	30 minutes
Whole buckwheat	3 cups	30 minutes
Whole barley	3 cups	20 minutes
Wild rice	3 cups	20 minutes
Brown rice	2 cups	20 minutes

Coat the pressure cooker with cooking oil or a nonstick vegetable oil spray to prevent sticking. Bring the water, milk, or broth to a boil and slowly add the grain. If desired, add ¼ to ½ tsp. salt for each cup of grain. Cover and bring to 15 pounds pressure, then reduce the heat so that the control knob jiggles only one to three times per minute. When the prescribed time elapses, reduce the pressure by dipping the pressure cooker into a pail of seawater (to save your freshwater supply).

Flavoring Suggestions for Cooked Whole Grains

Breakfast Grains
Sliced bananas
Crushed pineapple (stow small cans aboard)
Applesauce (use leftovers or small jars)
Raisins, dates, prunes, or dried apricots
Nuts
Sesame seeds
Sunflower seeds
Toasted wheat germ
Granola
Cinnamon, nutmeg, or ground cloves

Lunch or Dinner Grains
Cook in broth or bouillon instead of water
Onions, scallions, or chives
Carrots, celery, green peppers and mushrooms
Tomato paste, juice, or sauce
Garlic
Bay leaves
Black pepper
Basil, oregano, dill, tarragon, coriander, thyme, summer savory, sage, or marjoram
Lemon juice
Yogurt
Shredded cheese
Seeds or nuts
See pages 99–103 for additional dinner grain recipes.

DRY CEREALS

I feel that cooked whole grain cereals are the best choices nutritionally because it's always preferable to eat foods in their most basic, unprocessed form. But that doesn't mean that all commercial dry cereals are worthless. A number of them are quite commendable. Dry cereals are generally very low in fat, and some are fairly high in fiber. In addition, since they are usually eaten with milk, a dry cereal breakfast provides a good dose of calcium. For those people who don't allow themselves much time for breakfast, dry cereals are a good alternative to doughnuts.

In putting together the following list of recommended commercial dry cereals, I have used the following criteria:

- 6 grams or less of sucrose and other added sugars per serving
- 2 grams or less of fat per serving

Since 4 grams of sucrose or sugar equals 1 tsp. of sugar, a cereal with 6 grams of sucrose would have the equivalent of 1½ teaspoons of added sugar. If you compare the nutrition information panels on various boxes of cereals in the grocery store, you will see that the sugary "junk food" cereals for kids contain 12 to 16 grams of sugar per serving, or 3 to 4 spoonfuls of added sugar!

The only cereals that are over 2 grams of fat per serving are the granola types. It's OK to sprinkle them on top of dry cereals for a little extra flavor, but a whole bowl of granola will yield a substantial number of calories.

As far as fiber goes, look for more. Most cereals have about 2 grams of fiber per serving; I have placed an asterisk next to those recommended cereals that contain 4 grams or more per serving.

Most dry cereals contain a moderate amount of sodium (160–370 milligrams per serving). While this is not a problem for most people, those on low sodium diets might want to check the sodium content on the nutrition label. Shredded Wheat, Toasted Wheat & Raisins, Frosted Mini-Wheats, Puffed Wheat, and Puffed Rice contain almost no sodium, and Horizon Trail Mix Cereal is relatively low in sodium. (Whole grain, non-instant cooked cereals are extremely low in sodium.)

WHOLE WHEAT SESAME CEREAL

4 servings

This delicious hot cereal is ideal for people who like chewy whole grains. Whole wheat takes 3 to 4 hours to cook by the regular method, but only 30 minutes in a pressure cooker. The soy grits in this recipe are optional, enhancing the protein value.

I remember preparing this cereal during a cold, rainy day at the Isles of Shoals, New Hampshire. A hearty aroma filled the cabin as the wheat cooked, underscoring the snugness of our boat in the raw weather.

> 1½ c. whole wheat berries
> ¼ tsp. salt
> 4½ c. water
> 1½ Tbsp. soy grits (optional)
> 4 Tbsp. sesame seeds

1. In a pressure cooker, prepare the wheat according to the directions given on page 22.
2. After the wheat is cooked, add the soy grits and cook for 5 more minutes. (Add a little more water if the wheat is sticking to the pan.) Stir frequently to prevent sticking.
3. Just before serving, stir in the sesame seeds. Serve with skim milk and sweeten if desired.

1 serving = 224 calories

OAT BRAN CEREAL

2 servings

2 c. water
¼ tsp. salt (optional)
⅔ c. oat bran

1. In a saucepan, bring water and salt to a boil over high heat.
2. Stir in oat bran slowly (to avoid lumping) and constantly. Return to a boil, then reduce heat.
3. Cook for 1 to 2 minutes or until the desired consistency is reached, stirring frequently.

1 serving = 110 *calories*

GRANOLA SPLIT

1 serving

Rick and I once enjoyed this unusual, nutritious, and delightful breakfast at anchor in Horseshoe Cove, Maine, as we watched a group of harbor seals sunning themselves on a half-tide ledge. Since then, part of my pleasure in preparing this recipe comes from recalling that cruise.

1 banana
½ c. low-fat cottage cheese
¼ c. granola
¼ c. pineapple or other fruit

1. Halve banana lengthwise and place on a serving plate.
2. Spoon cottage cheese over the banana halves and sprinkle granola on top.
3. Top the sundae with pineapple or fruit of your choice.

1 serving = 349 *calories*

GRANOLA

7½ cups

This easy-to-make granola costs less and has less sugar and a more unsaturated type of fat than most store-bought granolas. I usually make it at home and keep a supply on the boat in an airtight container. It provides a tasty, fast, no-cook breakfast and is good alone with milk or added as a flavor and texture enhancer to other cereals. It also makes a great instant dessert when combined with yogurt, fruit, or both. It will keep for about a month without refrigeration.

> 4 c. rolled oats
> 1 c. wheat germ
> ½ c. sesame seeds
> ½ c. sunflower seeds
> ¼ c. honey, maple syrup, or brown sugar
> ¼ c. safflower oil
> 1 tsp. vanilla
> ½ c. raisins

1. In a large bowl, combine oats, sesame seeds, and sunflower seeds. Mix well.
2. In a small bowl, mix together sweetener, oil, and vanilla; add to dry ingredients and mix thoroughly.
3. Spread mixture on a cookie sheet or shallow baking pan.
4. Place in a 325° oven to bake for about 40 minutes or until golden brown. Stir every 10 minutes to prevent burning on the top and sides.
5. Add raisins and cool well. Store in an airtight container. To enhance fragrance, place a vanilla bean in the container.

¼ c. = 109 calories

(For variety, add other types of dried fruits and nuts. Go easy on coconut, however, because coconut contains a highly saturated fat.)

WHOLE WHEAT PANCAKES WITH BLUEBERRY SAUCE

4 servings

When blueberries are in season, try using this fruit sauce on your pancakes instead of maple syrup—to consume less sugar. The whole wheat pancakes help boost your fiber intake. The pancakes taste especially good if you add chopped peaches to the batter.

I like to serve these with Low Fat Sausage Patties, page 43.

WHOLE WHEAT PANCAKES

   1⅓ c. whole wheat flour
   2 tsp. baking powder
   1 Tbsp. packed brown sugar
   ¼ tsp. salt
   1 egg
   1⅓ c. skim milk
   1 Tbsp. oil
   2 or 3 chopped fresh or canned peaches (optional)

1. In a medium bowl, mix together flour, baking powder, brown sugar, and salt.
2. In a small bowl, use a fork to mix egg, milk, and oil.
3. Add wet ingredients to dry ingredients and stir only enough to moisten (batter should be slightly lumpy). If desired, stir in peaches.
4. For each pancake, pour about ¼ c. batter into a preheated lightly oiled or nonstick-sprayed frying pan. Cook until bubbles appear and edges are slightly dry. Flip pancakes and brown the other sides.
5. Serve with warm blueberry sauce (recipe follows).

1 *serving* = 251 *calories*

BLUEBERRY SAUCE

   2 tsp. cornstarch
   ½ c. water
   ¾ c. crushed fresh blueberries (1¼ c. whole)
   2 Tbsp. honey
   2 tsp. lemon juice

1. In a small saucepan, mix cornstarch with a small amount of the water until smooth.
2. Add remaining water, blueberries, and honey. Stir over medium heat until thickened and translucent.
3. Remove from heat; stir in lemon juice.
4. Serve warm over pancakes.

1 serving = 66 calories

OATMEAL-WHOLE WHEAT PANCAKES

4 servings

These pancakes are thicker and more filling than traditional pancakes because they are high in fiber from the oatmeal and whole wheat flour. As an added benefit, the oat bran in the oatmeal will help lower your cholesterol level.

> 1 c. whole wheat flour
> 1 tsp. baking soda
> 1 tsp. cream of tartar
> ½ tsp. salt
> 1 c. oatmeal
> 2 eggs
> 1 Tbsp. honey
> 1½ c. skim milk

1. In a large bowl, combine flour, baking soda, cream of tartar, salt, and oatmeal.
2. In a small bowl, use a fork to mix eggs, honey, and milk.
3. Add the wet ingredients to the dry ingredients and mix well. Let the mixture sit for about 5 minutes to allow the oatmeal to absorb the liquid.
4. Drop batter by spoonfuls into a preheated lightly oiled or nonstick-sprayed frying pan without crowding. When bubbles form, flip the pancakes and cook the other sides for 2 or 3 minutes.
5. Serve warm with margarine, syrup, honey, unsweetened apple-sauce, or other fruit sauces.

¼ recipes = 280 calories (not including toppings)

BANANA BRAN PANCAKES

4 servings

These high-fiber pancakes are low in sugar and so flavorful you can eat them without toppings. Kids love them.

1 c. whole wheat flour
½ c. unprocessed bran
1½ tsp. baking powder
a dash of salt
½ tsp. cinnamon
½ tsp. nutmeg
⅛ tsp. ground cloves
1 egg
1 tsp. oil
½ Tbsp. honey
1½ c. skim milk
½ tsp. vanilla extract
1 very ripe banana
½ c. finely chopped walnuts

1. In a large bowl, mix together the first seven ingredients until well blended.
2. In a small bowl, use a fork to mix egg, oil, honey, milk, and vanilla extract thoroughly.
3. Slice bananas in quarters lengthwise, then slice crosswise into very thin pieces.
4. Add egg mixture, banana, and walnuts to the flour mixture and stir until well blended. Add a little more milk if necessary, until the mixture has a pourable consistency.
5. Spoon batter into a preheated lightly oiled or nonstick-sprayed frying pan and cook until bubbles form; flip pancakes and cook other sides until golden brown.
6. Serve warm with or without toppings.

1 serving = 306 calories

WHOLE WHEAT
AND RAISIN GRIDDLE SCONES

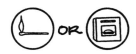

8 scones

I remember making these in the tiny, rockbound anchorage at Jewell Island, Maine. We were completely out of bread and were in the mood for it, so I started these cooking on the stovetop while we enjoyed the lovely scenery.

These easy and delightful scones can be either baked or cooked on a griddle or frying pan; leftovers can be reheated in the same way. Sometimes I keep all the ingredients on the boat; alternatively, I combine the dry ingredients in a jar at home and add the oil, milk, and raisins on the boat.

1 c. whole wheat flour
1 c. all-purpose flour
1 Tbsp. sugar
2 tsp. baking powder
¾ tsp salt
¼ tsp. baking soda
1 tsp. cinnamon
¼ c. safflower oil
¾ c. buttermilk (or ¾ c. skim milk plus 2 tsp. lemon juice or white vinegar)
½ c. raisins.

1. In a large bowl, mix together flours, sugar, baking powder, salt, baking soda, and cinnamon.
2. With a fork, cut in oil until the mixture resembles coarse crumbs.
3. Stir in buttermilk and raisins just until moistened.
4. With floured hands, pat dough onto a floured cutting board or countertop, forming a circle 9 inches in diameter and ½ inch thick.
5. Cut the dough circle into eight wedges and pull apart.
6. Fry wedges on a lightly oiled or nonstick-sprayed frying pan (you can also add a light coating of flour to further prevent sticking). Cook over low to medium heat for about 5 minutes or until the undersides are golden brown. Flip scones over and cook 4 to 5 minutes longer. (Alternatively, in a preheated 400° oven, bake on a lightly greased or nonstick-sprayed cookie sheet for 15 minutes or until lightly browned.)
7. Serve warm with jam or peanut butter if desired.

1 scone = 206 calories

CORNBREAD

9 servings

I can't begin to count the times I've made this recipe for sailing meals. If I'm having company aboard, I make it at home ahead of time to be **eaten with an egg recipe, bean soup, or chili. If we're on a vacation cruise, I sometimes make it on the boat when we're at anchor in some quiet cove.**

This recipe is very easy, moist, delicious, and healthy. Stored on the icebox shelf, it lasts up to 2 weeks.

> 1½ c. cornmeal
> ½ c. whole wheat flour
> ½ c. wheat germ
> ½ tsp. salt
> ½ tsp. baking soda
> 1 tsp. baking powder
> ¼ c. brown sugar
> 1 large egg, beaten with a fork
> 1 Tbsp. safflower oil
> 2 c. buttermilk (or 2 c. skim milk plus 2 Tbsp. lemon juice or vinegar)

1. In a large bowl, stir together the dry ingredients.
2. In another bowl, mix the wet ingredients.
3. Add the wet ingredients to the dry ingredients and stir until they are well mixed.
4. Pour the mixture into a lightly oiled or nonstick-sprayed 8-inch by 8-inch baking pan.
5. Bake in a preheated oven at 425° for 20 to 25 minutes.

1 serving = 170 calories

CORNMEAL PAN MUFFINS

6 servings

These quick and easy cakes are high in fiber and taste great with jam or peanut butter.

1½ c. hot water
2 c. cornmeal
½ c. unprocessed bran
¼ c. sugar
½ tsp. baking powder
½ tsp. baking soda

1. In a medium-sized bowl, combine all ingredients.
2. Shape into patties ½ inch thick.
3. Brown 10 minutes per side in a lightly oiled or nonstick-sprayed frying pan.

1 *serving* = 175 *calories*

CARROT-BRAN MUFFINS

2 dozen

These moist, delicious muffins are high in fiber and beta-carotene, substances believed to have cancer-fighting properties, and the molasses provides as much iron per muffin as a large egg. They're low in fat and calories and are great with peanut butter for breakfast. Store them in a lidded container in the icebox; they'll keep for about a week. If I make them at home, I put one dozen in the freezer and take the rest aboard.

2 c. whole wheat flour
2 c. unprocessed bran
1 tsp. salt
½ tsp. nutmeg
1½ tsp. cinnamon
2 tsp. baking soda
2½ Tbsp. vinegar
¼ c. safflower oil
¾ c. blackstrap molasses
2 eggs, beaten with a fork
2 c. skim milk
3 medium carrots, grated
½ c. raisins

1. In a large bowl, mix together the first six ingredients.
2. In a small bowl, mix together all remaining ingredients. (Measure oil first, then molasses in same measuring cup — molasses will slide right out.)
3. Combine wet and dry ingredients until moistened. Do not overmix.
4. Fill 24 lightly oiled or nonstick-sprayed muffin tins three-quarters full. Bake in a preheated 275° oven for 25 minutes or until an inserted toothpick comes out clean.

1 *muffin* = 117 *calories*

OATMEAL-OAT BRAN COFFEE CAKE

9 servings

Whenever I make this coffee cake, it reminds me of one of the more hair-raising sailing days I've ever been through. We had left Martha's Vineyard early that morning to head home, only to be hit by tropical disturbance Bob in Buzzards Bay. The VHF forecast had indicated 15-to 25-knot winds and rain, but when we got out onto the bay, the winds picked up to 40 knots. Our depth sounder stopped working and the mainsheet traveler car broke. The sky turned black, and rain came down in blinding sheets. Then the fog rolled in, blotting out our immediate surroundings, including the tugboat and barge that had been right behind us. Rather than continue our windward slog, we decided to turn back to the Vineyard. We got the mainsail down, lashed down the flailing boom, and set the storm jib, which pushed us at nearly 9 knots! We finally made it back to crowded Vineyard Haven Harbor and anchored in a tight berth given to us by the harbormaster. About an hour later, with the wind still howling, our anchor dragged, causing us to collide with a fishing boat. With the help of the boat's owner and the local marina, we pulled free and reanchored. Finally things settled down, but the day was a fizzle. I made this coffee cake and we curled up in warm bunks.

As coffee cakes go, you can't beat the nutrition in this one. It has plenty of soluble fiber, it's easy to make, very moist, and tastes great. By baking your own rather than buying one ready-made at the market, you are also cutting down significantly on saturated fats (for more information on saturated fats, see page 76).

CAKE

1 c. oat bran
1 c. oatmeal
⅓ c. firmly packed brown sugar
1 Tbsp. baking powder
¼ tsp. salt
1 tsp. cinnamon
1 egg, beaten with a fork
¼ c. safflower oil
1 c. skim milk
½ c. raisins
⅓ c. chopped walnuts

TOPPING

¼ c. brown sugar
1 Tbsp. flour
1 tsp. cinnamon
1 Tbsp. safflower oil

1. In a large bowl, combine the first six ingredients and mix well.
2. In a small bowl, mix together the egg, oil, and milk.
3. Add the wet ingredients to the dry ingredients and stir until combined. Stir in the raisins and walnuts.
4. Pour batter into a round or square baking pan that has been lightly oiled or nonstick-sprayed. Combine topping ingredients, and sprinkle it on top of the cake.
5. Bake at 400° for 20 to 25 minutes.

1 serving = 264 calories

OATMEAL-OAT BRAN MUFFINS

1. Follow the above recipe but pour batter into lightly oiled or nonstick-sprayed muffin tins. Omit topping.
2. Bake at 400° for 20 minutes or until golden brown.

1 muffin = 169 calories

PRESSURE-COOKED WHOLE WHEAT BREAD

1 loaf

Here is a great bread recipe for a pressure cooker. If you prefer to use an oven for this recipe, simply bake at 350° for 45 to 60 minutes. The first time I made this bread, I forgot to add the salt and it still tasted delicious. Try it that way if you have a crew member on a salt-restricted diet. This is a very simple recipe, one that can get you started using your pressure cooker for baking bread (you can bake other favorite yeast bread recipes in the same way). Stored in a plastic bag on the icebox shelf, this bread will keep for up to 2 weeks.

1¾ c. warm water plus 2 tsp. salt (or warm seawater and no salt)
3 Tbsp. brown sugar (or white sugar)
2 envelopes active dry yeast
2 Tbsp. safflower oil
3½ to 4 c. whole wheat flour

1. In a large bowl, combine warm water (105° to 115°, or about the temperature of bath water), salt, sugar, yeast, and oil. Mix well and let the mixture sit for a few minutes.
2. Stir in the flour, a cup at a time, until the batter is stiff. Use your hands to knead in the remaining flour until the dough no longer sticks to your fingers. Form into a ball.
3. Cover the bowl with a clean cloth, place in a warm spot (if you have an oven, you might turn it on for 3 minutes, then off), and let rise for 1 to 2 hours or until the dough has doubled in size.
4. Knead the dough well with floured hands and place in the pressure cooker after coating the cooker with oil or nonstick spray and covering its bottom with a sprinkling of oatmeal or cornmeal (to further prevent sticking).
5. Let dough rise again for 1 to 2 hours in the covered pressure cooker in a warm spot. Do not use the pressure regulator valve.
6. Place pressure cooker on a trivet over medium heat for 10 minutes, then turn heat to low and cook for about 50 to 60 minutes. Do not use the pressure regulator valve. When the bread is browned and pulling away from the edges, flip it over and cook for another 5 to 10 minutes to brown the top.

⅟₁₂ loaf = 169 calories

(For flavor variation, substitute other types of flour for one cup of the whole wheat flour. Use your imagination and add herbs, spices, raisins or other dried fruits, grated cheese, or onion bits to the bread dough.)

WHOLE WHEAT
IRISH SODA BREAD

1 loaf

This satisfying bread does not require the rising time of a yeast bread, yet is similar in consistency. I prefer it to yeast breads and think nothing of baking a loaf while we're on a sailing vacation. It requires only a few ingredients that can be stowed readily on a boat.

This bread can be baked either in an oven or in a pressure cooker, although the latter method takes longer. It tastes great with cheese or peanut butter, and the flavor can be varied by adding a half cup of raisins or currants, two tablespoons of poppy seeds, or a teaspoon of crushed caraway seeds to the dry ingredients.

If you store the bread on the shelf of your icebox, it should last for about 2 weeks.

2 c. whole wheat flour (plus about ½ c. more for kneading)
½ tsp. salt
1 tsp. baking soda
1 egg, beaten with a fork
3 Tbsp. honey
1 c. plain low-fat yogurt or buttermilk
  (or 1 c. skim milk plus 1 Tbsp. lemon juice or vinegar)
cornmeal or oatmeal (if using pressure cooker)

1. In a large bowl, combine the 2 c. whole wheat flour, salt, and baking soda.
2. In a small bowl, beat together the egg, honey, and yogurt or buttermilk.
3. Add the wet ingredients to the dry ingredients and stir well to mix the flour in. Add more flour to make a dough of kneadable consistency. If it is too dry, add more liquid; if too wet, add more flour.
4. Knead the dough for about 5 minutes, then shape into a flat, disk-shaped loaf.
5. Place the loaf on a lightly oiled or nonstick-sprayed baking sheet. Cut two parallel slashes into the dough to let it rise without cracking during baking.
6. Bake the bread at 375° for 25 to 30 minutes or until it is golden brown and an inserted toothpick comes out clean. Tap the bottom; if it sounds hollow, it's done. Alternatively, place the loaf in the bottom of a pressure cooker that has been oiled and sprinkled with oatmeal

or cornmeal. Place the covered pressure cooker on a trivet over medium heat for 10 minutes, then turn the heat to low and cook for about 50 to 60 minutes. Do not use the pressure regulator valve. When the bread is browned and pulling away from the edges, flip it over and cook for another 5 to 10 minutes to brown the top.

⅒ loaf = 134 calories without raisins or currants
155 calories with raisins or currants

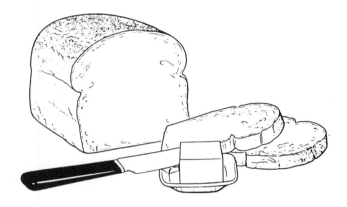

WHOLE WHEAT
IRISH SODA BREAD
WITH WHEAT SPROUTS

1 loaf

To make this variation on the foregoing recipe, start sprouting wheat berries 4 or 5 days prior to baking the bread. The sprouts add a nice heartiness to this delicious, easy bread.

1. See pages 48–49 for instructions on sprouting grains. Start with ⅓ c. whole wheat berries, which sprout to a length of only ¼ inch.
2. Chop the sprouts and add to the wet ingredients in the above recipe.

⅒ loaf = 155 calories without raisins or currants
176 calories with raisins or currants

EASIER AND HEALTHIER EGGS BENEDICT

2 servings

Since eggs are high in cholesterol, it's considered prudent to limit your egg yolk consumption to two per week. When you do decide to indulge, this delicious recipe is not only easier than its traditional counterpart but also healthier because the sauce contains less cholesterol than hollandaise sauce. I prepare this often when I want to enjoy an elegant breakfast at the cockpit table.

> 2 slices pumpernickel bread
> 2 slices very lean pre-cooked ham, unheated
> 2 eggs
> 1 Tbsp. lemon juice
> 2 Tbsp. mayonnaise

1. In a small bowl, whisk together lemon juice and mayonnaise. (A small wire whisk does the job nicely.)
2. Place 1 slice of pumpernickel bread on each serving plate; place 1 slice of ham on bread; top ham with 1 poached or soft-boiled egg.
3. Spoon sauce on top of each egg. Serve with sliced tomatoes, if desired, and some fresh parsley.

1 serving = 275 *calories*

ARTICHOKE-CHEESE SCRAMBLE

8 servings

This is a great "company" recipe — rich, filling, and unique! We enjoyed this with friends during a brisk September sail on the Sakonnet River in Rhode Island, while pausing in a beautiful anchorage tucked into the colorful, tree-lined riverbank.

3 jars (6 oz. each) marinated artichoke hearts, chopped
3 bunches green onions, chopped (1½ c.)
1 clove garlic, chopped
8 eggs
10 soda crackers, crumbled
⅛ c. parsley flakes
1 lb. cheddar cheese, shredded
a dash of liquid hot pepper seasoning
a dash of Worcestershire sauce
¼ tsp. black pepper

1. Drain the oil from the artichokes, reserving 2 Tbsp. Place the 2 Tbsp. oil in a large frying pan and add the onions and garlic. Cook until onions are limp.
2. In a large bowl, beat eggs with a fork. Add cracker crumbs and beat again.
3. Stir in remaining ingredients, including onions and garlic.
4. Pour mixture back into the large frying pan and scramble over low heat until done.
5. Serve with a bread of your choice and a fruit or juice.

1 *serving* = 400 *calories*

CURRIED SCRAMBLED EGGS

2 servings

My husband Rick invented this quick and wonderful recipe while experimenting with spices one Saturday morning. If you like the taste of curry, you will be amazed at what it does for scrambled eggs. Very filling, too!

3 *eggs*
2 *oz. sharp cheddar cheese, or cheese of your choice, grated*
2 *Tbsp. water*
3 *dashes curry powder*
1 *dash cayenne powder*
2 *dashes black pepper*
2 *dashes parsley flakes*

1. In a small bowl, mix all ingredients together with a fork. Be creative and use spices as your tastes dictate.
2. Scramble mixture over low heat in a lightly oiled or nonstick-sprayed frying pan.
3. Serve with pan-toasted whole wheat bagels or English muffins and a refreshing glass of orange juice.

1 *serving* = 220 *calories*

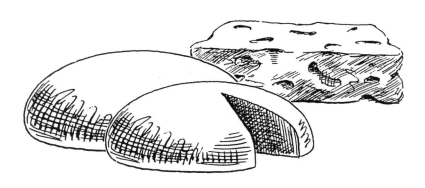

LOW-FAT "SAUSAGE" PATTIES

12 patties

Traditional sausage patties are very high in fat, but you can enjoy the same taste in my reduced-fat version. I like to serve them with pancakes, and they have received rave reviews.

1 lb. lean hamburger
2 Tbsp. fennel seed
2 Tbsp. anise seed
½ tsp. cayenne pepper
1 tsp. salt
¼ tsp. hot pepper flakes
2 Tbsp. maple syrup (optional)

1. Mix all ingredients together in a bowl and shape into 12 disk-shaped patties.
2. Brown patties on both sides in a lightly oiled or nonstick-sprayed frying pan and serve.

1 patty = 78 calories

3

LUNCH

Lunch is a meal that varies from sailor to sailor and from situation to situation. Sometimes you find yourself sailing right through lunch, while at other times you're ready to stop and relax. In this chapter I have included some easy, no-cook recipes such as salads and sandwiches that you can make in a flash while sailing. But I have also included some more elaborate foods such as Whole Wheat Pizza (page 59) and Mexican Munchies (page 61) for those times when you anchor for a leisurely lunchbreak.

Even a quick lunch can be delicious and nutritionally satisfying. I remember one lunch I made while we were pounding along en route to Nantucket with vacationing friends. I prepared the tuna salad for Tuna Salad in Cantaloupe Bowls (page 50) soon after leaving port so that it would be chilled for lunch. When lunchtime rolled around, I simply filled the cantaloupe halves with the tuna and served whole grain crackers on the side. We enjoyed this refreshing and very healthy lunch in the cockpit under clear blue skies and puffy clouds.

Whatever your sailing plans, you should find a recipe in this chapter to suit your sailing needs. Since typical sailing lunches are high in calories, I have featured recipes that include a lot of fruits and vegetables. Whenever possible, I have tried to use yogurt for all or part of the mayonnaise in a recipe, a tasty substitution that substantially decreases the fat content and calories. I have also included some tips on how to select the leanest sandwich fillings — although with all the other tasty menu items to choose from, you may find yourself losing interest in sandwiches!

HOW TO CHOOSE THE BEST SANDWICH FILLINGS

Use the accompanying chart to help compare some of the more popular sandwich fillings. Foods are listed from lowest to highest in fat content; generally, the lower the fat, the lower the calories. In fact, fat has more than twice as many calories as an equal amount of protein or carbohydrate—9 per gram, as opposed to 4 for protein and carbohydrate. (For more information on fat and cholesterol, see page 74.)

Your best bet for choosing lean sandwich fillings is simply to look for pure meat or poultry where you can see the grain of the meat. That way you know you are not getting any added "mystery fat."

Many people believe that "all beef" frankfurters are lean, but they are actually very high in "all beef" fat. A 1½-ounce frankfurter contains 141 calories; of that total, 117 calories come from fat. You may think that frankfurters are a good, inexpensive protein meal, but you are really paying a high price for salted, flavored fat! It's a better buy to pay more for the lean, pure meats that provide more protein and less fat.

When I plan my lunch menus, I choose Swiss cheese quite often. Although cheese is high in fat, its redeeming quality is that it is also high in calcium—particularly Swiss cheese.

COMPARATIVE FAT AND CALORIE CONTENT OF SANDWICH FILLINGS

Perishable Foods

Food (1 oz.)	Calories	Fat (grams)
Ham, 95% fat free, cooked	35	1
Chicken breast, no skin, cooked	45	1
Turkey breast, no skin, cooked	45	1
Turkey ham	35	2
Roast beef, lean, cooked	69	3.8
Mozzarella cheese, part-skim	72	4.1
Ham, deli-style, cooked	65	5
Salami, cooked	90	7
Peanut butter, 1 Tbsp. (½ oz.)	86	7.2
Swiss cheese	107	7.8
Bologna	85	8
Liverwurst	90	8
Cheddar cheese	114	9.4
Salami, hard	135	12
Frankfurter (1½ oz.)	141	13

Nonperishable Foods

Food	Calories	Fat
Shrimp, canned	33	.3
Tuna, water-packed	36	.6
Salmon, pink, canned	46	2.3
Chicken, canned, boneless	50	2.8
Turkey, canned, boneless	50	2.8
Sardines, canned in oil, drained	58	3
Corned beef, canned	67	3.8
Deviled meat spreads	75	6
Tuna, packed in oil	85	6.5
Ham, canned	87	7.5
Vienna sausage, canned	90	8.5

BETA-CAROTENE
AND
VITAMIN A

Lunch and dinner are good meals in which to include foods high in beta-carotene and vitamin A. Beta-carotene is converted to vitamin A after consumption, and vitamin A is needed for good night vision, healthy skin and bones, and healing of wounds. Beta-carotene has also been shown to be associated with lower rates of most cancers. Both nutrients are generally found in dark green or deep orange or yellow vegetables. The darker the color, the higher the beta-carotene content. So, do yourself a favor and choose plenty of fruits and vegetables from the opposite column, listed from highest to lowest as good sources of vitamin A and beta-carotene. Asterisks indicate foods that are easily stored on your boat (for specific storage suggestions, see pages 9–11). Items without asterisks need to be eaten quickly. You will find many delicious recipes in this cookbook that contain these very beneficial and healthful foods.

Carrots*
Pumpkin*
Spinach[1]
Butternut squash*
Hubbard squash*
Sweet potatoes*
Cantaloupe*
Turnip greens
Kale
Mustard greens
Beet greens
Bok choy
Papaya
Broccoli
Red peppers*
Apricots[1]
Dried apricots*
Nectarines*
Acorn squash*
Romaine lettuce
Peaches[1]
Asparagus[1]
Tomatoes*
Prunes*
Grapefruit*
Watermelon*
Peas[1]
Green peppers*
Oranges*
Brussels sprouts
Lima beans[1]
Bananas*
Pineapple*
Cabbage*

[1]*easily stored if canned*

MAKE YOUR OWN SPROUTS

Once your fresh vegetables are gone, you may crave something crunchy and fresh. Sprouts are the easy answer. The major nutritional advantage of sprouts is their contribution of vitamin C to your diet. Raw sprouts contain between 9 and 20 milligrams of vitamin C per cup (the recommended dietary allowance for vitamin C is 60 milligrams per day). You lose about two-thirds of the vitamin C by cooking the sprouts, so it's best to eat them raw.

Sprouts are great in place of lettuce in sandwiches and salads, and wheat sprouts can be chopped up and used in bread recipes to add a nice chewiness to the bread (see page 39).

What To Sprout

You can buy seeds and beans for sprouting at health food stores; occasionally you'll also find them in supermarkets. Beware of buying seeds at nurseries or farm supply stores; these seeds may have been chemically treated for planting!

Seeds for sprouting:
alfalfa
chia
radish
mustard
garden cress

Grains and beans for sprouting:
wheat berries
rye
mung beans
lentils
whole dried peas and lima beans
soybeans

How To Sprout

Day 1: Soak 1 Tbsp. of seeds or ⅓ c. of beans or grains in 1 quart of water overnight.
Day 2: Rinse seeds thoroughly and drain well. Place in a quart-sized canning jar with a screen cut to fit the top of the jar under the canning ring. Store jar in a dark cupboard on its side in a large bowl to collect any drainage. Try to flush the sprouts with fresh water every 4 to 6 hours or at least twice daily. Make sure to drain the sprouts well each time.
Day 3: Continue to rinse and drain the sprouts. Discard any seeds that have not started sprouting and have fallen to the bottom of the jar.
Day 4: Wheat and rye sprouts are ready to eat.
Day 5: Mung bean, lentil, pea, soybean and lima sprouts are ready to eat.
Day 6: Alfalfa, radish, mustard, garden cress and chia sprouts are usually ready to eat.

Store sprouts in an airtight container in your icebox or use as soon as they are ready if you have no ice. Refrigerated sprouts will keep for up to several weeks.

To increase the vitamin C content of your sprouts, place them in the sun for a few hours to turn them green before refrigerating.

TUNA SALAD
IN CANTALOUPE BOWLS

4 servings

This beautiful, refreshing dish is high in beta-carotene, vitamin C, protein, and fiber. You can save calories by substituting yogurt for part or all of the mayonnaise if you'd like. Serve with Carrot-Bran Muffins (page 34) for an added fiber and vitamin boost.

2 cans (7 oz.) water-packed tuna, drained and flaked
3 stalks celery, sliced
⅓ c. mayonnaise or plain low-fat yogurt
4 Tbsp. fresh lemon or lime juice (2 lemons or limes)
⅛ tsp. pepper
2 large, ripe, chilled cantaloupes, halved and seeded

1. Combine tuna, celery, mayonnaise or yogurt, 2 Tbsp. lemon or lime juice and pepper. Cover and chill.
2. Just before serving, sprinkle cantaloupes with 1 Tbsp. lemon or lime juice and fill with tuna salad. Sprinkle remaining 1 Tbsp. lemon or lime juice on top of tuna salad and serve.

1 serving = 342 calories with mayonnaise
217 calories with yogurt

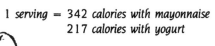

CHERRY-NUT CHICKEN SALAD

4 servings

Try this delightful chicken salad when cherries are in season, or use grapes instead of cherries. Serve with whole grain crackers or muffins, and for a special treat, serve in cantaloupe halves. I usually make the chicken salad at home, transport it to the boat in a Tupperware container, and store it down on the ice.

1½ c. cooked, cubed chicken or 2 cans (5 oz. each) chunk white chicken
½ c. plain low-fat yogurt or mayonnaise
2 c. fresh cherries or grapes, halved and pitted
¼ c. chopped walnuts
salt and pepper to taste

Combine all ingredients and chill until serving time, if you have ice.

1 serving = 400 calories with mayonnaise
210 calories with plain yogurt

APPLE-CHEESE TOSS

6 servings

You can put this together on a calm day at sea when you're tired of sandwiches. I made this when we were having a gentle sail to Shelter Island, N.Y., and it was no trouble at all to make while underway. Serve with crunchy whole wheat crackers or a whole grain bread or muffin.

4 medium apples, cut in chunks
6 oz. cubed cheddar or Muenster cheese
½ c. raisins
¼ c. chopped walnuts
2 Tbsp. lemon juice
½ c. mayonnaise
¾ c. orange juice
Lettuce leaves (optional)

1. In a medium-sized bowl, whisk together the lemon juice, mayonnaise and orange juice.
2. Add the apples, cheese, raisins and walnuts; mix well and serve on a bed of lettuce, if desired.

1 serving = 384 calories

THREE BEAN
AND CHEESE SALAD

4 servings

This is a great meal to make when your fresh supplies run out. I usually keep the ingredients on hand for a meal toward the end of our cruise. This lunch entree is high in fiber and low in fat. It takes only minutes to prepare, but it's best if made ahead of time so that the flavors blend. I usually make it on the boat in the morning—either before we sail or during the sail. Serve with whole grain crackers and fruit.

1 can (16 oz.) vegetarian-style beans in tomato sauce
1 can (8 oz.) cut green beans, drained
1 can (8½ oz.) lima beans, drained
3 oz. diced cheddar cheese
1 small onion, chopped
1 Tbsp. parsley flakes
2 tsp. crushed basil leaves
2 tsp. lemon juice
a generous dash of pepper

1. In a medium-sized bowl, combine all ingredients.
2. Cover and chill, if you have ice, for at least 2 hours to blend flavors, stirring occasionally.

1 serving = 250 calories

LEMONY TUNA AND BEANS

6 servings

This is another dish that is great for when your fresh foods run low. It's easy to make, filling, high in fiber and low in cholesterol. Serve on lettuce leaves (if you have them) with crunchy, whole grain crackers. It tastes best if allowed to chill before serving.

1 *can (16 oz.) cut green beans, drained*
1 *can (8 oz.) green lima beans, drained*
1 *can (15 oz.) garbanzo beans (chick peas), drained*
1 *can (7 oz.) water-packed tuna, drained*
2 *large stalks celery, chopped*
½ *c. mayonnaise or plain low-fat yogurt*
¼ *c. lemon juice (2 lemons)*
1 *Tbsp. chopped onion*
½ *tsp. lemon pepper seasoning*
⅛ *tsp. garlic powder*
lettuce leaves (optional)

1. Combine all ingredients except the lettuce in a large bowl.
2. Cover and chill until serving time, if you have ice; serve on a bed of lettuce, if desired

1 *serving* = 309 *calories with mayonnaise*
        184 *calories with yogurt*

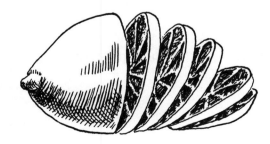

CRUSTLESS SPINACH PIE

6 servings

This is one of my favorite lunch recipes. You can serve it hot or cold; I usually make it ahead of time and serve it cold with a fruit salad. This recipe is very high in protein, iron, calcium, vitamin A and beta-carotene. It is also relatively low in fat since there is no pie crust. If you don't like spinach, you can substitute broccoli.

1 *package (10 oz.) frozen chopped spinach or broccoli, thawed and well drained (or use fresh spinach or broccoli, cooked, well drained, and chopped)*
½ *lb. sharp cheddar or feta cheese, grated or crumbled*
2 *c. low-fat cottage cheese*
4 *eggs*
6 *Tbsp. flour*
¼ *tsp. salt*
½ *tsp. pepper*

1. In a medium-sized bowl, combine spinach, grated cheese and cottage cheese.
2. In a small bowl, mix eggs with a fork and add the flour, salt and pepper.
3. Combine both mixtures and mix well.
4. Place mixture in a lightly oiled or nonstick-sprayed pie pan, and bake for 1 hour at 350°.

1 *serving* = 283 *calories*

SPINACH PIE WITH YOGURT

6 servings

This recipe is lighter than the above recipe and can be made with or without a crust. It's very low in calories if you omit the crust, and it can be served either hot or cold. This recipe is also very high in calcium, iron, vitamin A and beta-carotene and is a high-quality protein dish. (Broccoli may be substituted for the spinach.)

1 *partly-baked whole wheat pie crust (optional, recipe follows)*
2 *eggs, beaten with a fork*
1 *c. plain low-fat yogurt*
1 *package (10 oz.) frozen chopped spinach or broccoli, thawed and*
  well drained (or use fresh spinach or broccoli, cooked, well drained, and
  chopped)
salt and pepper to taste
2 *Tbsp. chopped onion*
1 *c. grated cheddar cheese (or cheese of your choice)*

1. If you are using a pie crust, follow the recipe for Whole Wheat Pie Crust (below).
2. In a medium-sized bowl, combine eggs and yogurt. Add spinach and salt and pepper to taste.
3. Place onion and cheese in the bottom of the pie crust or a nonstick-sprayed pie pan. Add spinach mixture.
4. Bake at 425° for 15 minutes, then at 350° for 30 minutes.

1 *serving* = 110 *calories without crust*
            260 *calories with crust*

WHOLE WHEAT PIE CRUST

1 bottom shell

You could save time by buying a prepared, frozen crust instead of making your own, but the advantage of making your own is that you get a delicious whole wheat flavor and avoid the hydrogenated saturated fats found in prepared pie crusts (see page 76).

> 1 c. whole wheat flour
> ¼ tsp. salt
> ¼ c. safflower oil
> 4 Tbsp. ice water (if available)

1. In a medium-sized bowl, combine flour and salt. Add oil and water and mix lightly with a fork until the pastry leaves the sides of the bowl clean. Knead with hands until the dough holds together into a ball.
2. Roll out into a pie pan-sized circle between 2 pieces of waxed paper and fit into a pie pan. Press and shape the dough into the pie pan and flute to make a scalloped edge. Prick the crust all over with a fork.
3. For quiches, bake the pie crust for 8 minutes at 425° (this prevents it from getting soggy during the further baking of the quiche). If a pre-baked pie shell is required for other recipes, bake at 425° for 15 minutes, or until the pastry is lightly browned.

⅙th of pie crust = 150 calories

SUMMER SQUASH AND CHEESE QUICHE

6 servings

This easy recipe provides a great way to use summer squash when it is plentiful. It can be served hot or cold and goes well with sliced tomatoes and fresh whole grain bread. Prepare it ahead of time for lunch when you're in a hurry. (Quiches will keep for several days aboard when covered with foil and stored down on the ice.)

I remember making this for a picnic lunch at a secluded beach in Bermuda. We sipped wine, ate quiche, and enjoyed gazing at the incredibly vivid surroundings—pink sand, blue sky and crystal clear turquoise water.

1 lb. summer squash (green or yellow)
½ tsp. salt (to sprinkle on the squash)
4 eggs, beaten with a fork
8 oz. grated Swiss or Monterey Jack cheese
1 tsp. basil, dill, oregano or tarragon
¼ c. freshly grated parmesan cheese

1. Grate squash coarsely into a medium-sized bowl. Sprinkle with the salt and let stand for 10 minutes. Squeeze out all liquid.
2. Add eggs, cheese (not parmesan), and seasoning to the squash.
3. Pour mixture into a lightly oiled or nonstick-sprayed pie pan or baking dish and top with the parmesan cheese.
4. Bake at 350° for 30 to 40 minutes or until quiche is set in the center and the edges are lightly browned.

1 serving = 222 calories

INCREDIBLY SIMPLE TUNA PIE

6 servings

This pie takes only minutes to prepare and is good hot or cold. I like to serve it cold for lunch with Carrot-Raisin Salad (page 113) and whole grain bread or muffins.

2 (7½ oz.) cans water-packed tuna
4 oz. (1 c.) shredded part-skim mozzarella cheese
½ c. chopped onion
2 eggs
½ c. mayonnaise or plain low-fat yogurt
¼ c. skim milk

1. Combine all ingredients and place in a lightly oiled or nonstick-sprayed pie plate.
2. Bake at 400° for 20 to 25 minutes or until lightly browned. Serve hot or cold.

1 serving = 294 calories with mayonnaise
             167 calories with yogurt

CHILLED SESAME LINGUINE

8 servings

This delightful and very unusual dish makes a great lunch combined with fresh fruit salad. Add a quiche if you have a very hungry crew. I usually prepare it ahead of time and add scallions before serving.

1 lb. thin linguine (#17) or spaghetti
2 Tbsp. sesame or peanut oil
1 Tbsp. minced fresh gingerroot
4 tsp. sugar
¼ c. sesame tahini or creamy peanut butter
¼ c. soy sauce
2 Tbsp. wine vinegar
¼ tsp. crushed red pepper flakes
2 scallions, cut into 2-inch pieces

1. Cook linguine according to the label directions in a large pot; drain. Toss with sesame oil and chill until cold, if you have an icebox; or let cool.
2. In a small bowl, using a wire whisk, combine ginger with remaining ingredients except scallions. Pour over chilled linguine.
3. Before serving, toss well and sprinkle scallions over the top.

1 *serving* = 296 *calories*

BABAGANOUJ

1 small bowl

I like to serve this Near Eastern recipe with Hummus (recipe follows), Syrian bread triangles, and raw vegetable and fruit slices. Place everything on your cockpit table and let everyone dig in! You can prepare both recipes up to 2 days ahead of time and chill until serving time. I usually make these at home, then store down on the ice in Tupperware containers.

1 1 lb. eggplant
3 Tbsp. sesame tahini
2 cloves garlic, minced
3 Tbsp. lemon juice

1. Bake the eggplant at 350° for 1 hour.
2. Place baked eggplant in a large bowl and remove skin (be careful not to burn yourself as the hot steam escapes). Mash well with a fork and blend in the remaining ingredients. Chill if you have ice, or let cool before serving.

Entire recipe = 400 calories

HUMMUS

1 small bowl

Follow the same recipe as above but substitute 1 can (15 oz.) garbanzo beans (chick-peas), partially drained and well mashed, for the eggplant. Serve as is or chilled.

Entire recipe = 807 calories

WHOLE WHEAT PIZZA

8 servings

If you've never tried whole wheat pizza before, you're in for a tasty surprise! This is a good recipe to try when you and your guests have anchored for a leisurely lunchbreak. It's satisfying enough to be a festive dinner, too. I remember making it on the boat one balmy July night with weekend guests aboard. It was really fun eating pizza under the stars!

If you prefer to omit the ground beef, you can add more vegetables to the topping—or use your imagination! Sometimes I cook the ground beef, onion, garlic and tomato puree at home beforehand; at lunch time all I need to do is heat it up and add the vegetables and spices.

(When you're in the mood for pizza and don't have time to make this recipe, you might want to try my quick and easy English Muffin Pizzas, page 151.)

CRUST

1 c. warm water (not hot)
1 envelope active dry yeast
1 tsp. honey
1 Tbsp. safflower oil
½ tsp. salt
2 c. whole wheat flour (plus about ½ c. more to form the dough)

TOPPING

1 lb. lean ground beef
1 onion, chopped
1 clove garlic, minced
2 c. tomato puree or sauce
1 green pepper, sliced
½ lb. mushrooms, sliced
½ tsp. each basil, oregano and black pepper
⅛ tsp. crushed red pepper flakes (if you like it spicy-hot)
salt to taste
8 oz. part-skim mozzarella cheese, shredded

1. In a large saucepan, begin cooking ground beef, onion and garlic.
2. In a medium-sized bowl, combine warm water, yeast, honey, oil and salt for the crust. Let stand for 5 minutes.
3. After the beef is cooked, drain grease and add the remaining topping ingredients (except cheese) and simmer while the crust is being prepared.
4. Add flour to the yeast mixture and beat dough until it is smooth and elastic. Add about ½ c. more flour or enough to make a stiff dough. Turn dough onto a floured surface and knead until smooth. Stretch dough onto a lightly oiled or nonstick-sprayed cookie sheet or a large, rectangular, shallow pan. Form edges on outer sides of crust.
5. Spread topping (except cheese) over dough and bake at 450° for 15 minutes, or until bottom of crust is crisp.
6. Sprinkle cheese over the top and heat until the cheese has just melted. Serve piping hot.

⅛th of pizza = 374 calories

MEXICAN MUNCHIES

I like to serve Tacos and Bean-Cheese Tortillas for a festive, leisurely lunch. You can vary the fillings considerably according to your preferences and what's available.

TACOS

Buy prepared taco shells and stuff them with Mexican-seasoned, cooked ground beef (see recipe below) or refried beans. Heat the stuffed tacos in your oven at about 350° for 10 to 15 minutes or until the filling is warm; then melt Monterey Jack or sharp cheddar cheese on top. Serve with any or all of the following toppings:
Mexican salsa
Mexican hot sauce
chopped onions or scallions
chopped tomatoes
chopped red or green peppers
shredded lettuce
guacamole (see recipe, page 153)
chopped green chilies

BEAN-CHEESE TORTILLAS

Buy prepared tortillas and spread with a layer of refried beans, then a layer of Mexican Hot Sauce; top with Monterey Jack or sharp cheddar cheese. Broil until cheese melts. Cut tortillas into small triangles and serve hot. (This makes a good appetizer too!)

SEASONED BEEF

1 lb. lean ground beef
1 large onion, chopped
1–2 garlic cloves, minced
1 can (6 oz.) tomato paste plus 1 can of water
1 can (4 oz.) chopped green chilies (optional but good!)
2 Tbsp. chili powder
1 tsp. cumin
1 tsp. oregano
½ tsp. coriander
a splash of hot pepper sauce
salt and pepper to taste

1. Brown ground beef in a large frying pan with onion and garlic; drain grease.
2. Add remaining ingredients and simmer for about 15 minutes. If you don't have all the seasonings just improvise—it will still taste great!

1 taco stuffed with ⅒th of above recipe and ½ oz. cheese = 202 calories

LENTIL SOUP

8 *servings*

Lentils are very high in fiber and will provide complete protein when eaten with grains, seeds, or dairy products. (What's complete protein? See page 94.) This recipe is particularly tasty served with whole grain bread and a wedge of cheese. It is easy to make, either in a pressure cooker or by regular stovetop cooking. For more information on cooking beans, see page 97.

2½ c. lentils (1 lb.)
2 qts. water
1 large onion, chopped
3 carrots, chopped
2 large stalks celery, chopped
1 clove garlic, chopped
3 bay leaves
¼ tsp. pepper
½ tsp. thyme
1 Tbsp. parsley flakes
salt to taste

Pressure Cooker Method

1. Soak lentils in plenty of water for at least 6 hours or overnight. (You may want to use seawater.)
2. Drain lentils, then combine them with the water and all other ingredients in a pressure cooker.
3. Cover, set the control knob at 15 pounds pressure and cook for 20 minutes after the control knob jiggles. Adjust heat so that the control jiggles 1 to 3 times a minute.
4. Allow the cooker to cook on the stovetop for 5 minutes, then place it in a bucket of sea water to reduce pressure.

Regular Cooking Method

Soak lentils as indicated above; combine all ingredients in a large cooking pot and bring to a boil; reduce heat and simmer 40 to 50 minutes or until tender.

1 serving = 209 calories

FOOD STORAGE TIP:
STORING FOOD IN YOUR PRESSURE COOKER

If you have leftover soup, you don't have to bother transferring it to another container to store in the icebox. Simply cover the pressure cooker and bring the soup to 15 pounds pressure. Then turn off the heat and leave the cooker right on the stovetop. The food inside will remain "preserved" until you open the cooker. Some sailors use this method to keep a continual soup pot going—adding new ingredients or leftovers daily as they become available.

CABBAGE-CHEDDAR CHOWDER

8 servings

I made this chowder when we arrived home from a very cold and rainy sail across Buzzards Bay. It was one of those days where you keep getting buckets of water poured on your head and down your neck. I must admit I enjoy the excitement of that type of sailing—struggling at the wheel to compensate for gusts of wind and rolling waves. But after you've been soaked and pounded for a while, you do get pretty cold and tired. A hot, hearty chowder is hard to beat!

This chowder is easy to make and is great for either lunch or dinner with apple slices and whole grain bread. Both cabbage and green peppers are high in vitamin C, beta-carotene and fiber. The cheese and milk add significant amounts of calcium.

1 *lb. lean ground beef (optional)*
2 *medium stalks celery, sliced*
1 *small onion, chopped*
1 *medium green pepper, chopped*
1 *medium head cabbage, coarsely shredded*
½ *c. water*
3 *c. skim milk*
2 *c. (8 oz.) shredded cheddar cheese*
3 *Tbsp. flour*
1 *tsp. salt*
⅛ *tsp. ground nutmeg*
¼ *tsp. black pepper*

1. In a large pot, cook and stir the ground beef, celery, onion and green pepper until the vegetables are tender. Drain grease from pan.
2. Stir in cabbage and water; cover and cook over low heat, stirring occasionally, until cabbage is tender, about 10 minutes.
3. Stir in milk, cheese, flour, salt, nutmeg and pepper. Heat to boiling, stirring constantly. Boil and stir 1 minute, then serve.

1 *serving* = 258 *calories with beef*
156 *calories without beef*

CHILI CORN CHOWDER

6 servings

Green chilies make this chowder more lively than a traditional corn chowder. It's quick and easy but very satisfying. Serve with whole grain bread and a fruit and cheese platter.

1 tsp. safflower oil
1 medium onion, chopped
¼ lb. small mushrooms, sliced thin, or 1 can (4 oz.) sliced mushrooms, drained
1 large potato, diced
½ c. water
1 can (17 oz.) cream-style corn
1 can condensed cream of mushroom soup
2 c. skim milk
½ tsp. salt
1 can (4 oz.) green chilies, seeded and chopped

1. In a large pot, stir-fry onion, mushrooms and potato in oil for about 5 minutes or until golden. Stir in water; cover and simmer for 15 minutes or until potato is tender.
2. Add corn, soup, milk and salt and bring just to boiling. Stir in chilies, lower heat and simmer for about 5 minutes, then serve.

1 serving = 180 calories

OPEN-FACED
MOZZARELLA AND PEPPERS

4 servings

4 slices whole grain bread
4 green pepper rings
4 oz. part-skim mozzarella cheese, sliced
1 large roast pepper or pimiento, quartered
1 Tbsp. vinegar
½ tsp. oregano

1. On each slice of bread layer green pepper, mozzarella and roast pepper. Sprinkle each with vinegar and oregano.
2. Broil or heat in a frying pan until cheese melts (or eat cold).

1 serving = 170 calories

OPEN-FACED REUBENS

4 servings

1 Tbsp. mayonnaise
1 Tbsp. catsup
4 slices rye bread
4 oz. thinly sliced corned beef
2 c. sauerkraut, well drained
4 oz. Swiss cheese, sliced

1. Mix together mayonnaise and catsup and spread on bread. Top with corned beef and sauerkraut; cover with cheese.
2. Broil for about 5 minutes or until cheese is lightly browned and melted (or heat in a frying pan until cheese is melted).

1 serving = 284 calories

APPLE-CHEDDAR BROIL

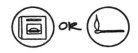

4 servings

4 English muffins, split
4 oz. (1 c.) cheddar cheese, shredded
½ c. applesauce
cinnamon

1. Toast muffins in broiler or on a frying pan.
2. Combine cheese and applesauce and spread over each muffin half.
   Sprinkle with cinnamon.
3. Broil or heat in a frying pan until bubbly and lightly browned.

1 serving = 280 calories

CANNED CORNED BEEF
AND CHEESE SANDWICHES

8 servings

1 can (12 oz.) corned beef, crumbled
1 small onion, chopped
1½ Tbsp. chopped dill pickle (optional)
¼–½ tsp. hot pepper sauce
½ c. catsup
6 oz. diced cheese
8 whole grain hamburger buns or 16 slices whole grain bread

1. In a large bowl combine all ingredients and spread the mixture on
   the hamburger buns or bread slices.
2. Wrap each bun or sandwich in foil, place on a baking sheet and bake
   at 350° for about 20 minutes or until heated through.

1 serving = 336 calories

NUTTY EGG AND
GREEN BEAN SANDWICHES

4 servings

This is a delightfully unusual vegetarian sandwich—good for when you're out of fresh foods.

½ c. walnuts, finely chopped
1 medium onion, finely diced
1 can (16 oz.) French-style green beans, drained and diced
2 hard-boiled eggs, finely chopped
2 Tbsp. peanut butter
2 Tbsp. mayonnaise
8 slices pumpernickel or whole wheat bread
lettuce leaves (optional)

1. In a medium-sized bowl, combine walnuts, onion, green beans and eggs.
2. In a cup, mix together peanut butter and mayonnaise until smooth and add to the green bean mixture.
3. Spread green bean mixture on 4 bread slices, then top with lettuce and remaining bread slices.

1 serving = 390 calories

CRABMEAT SUPREME
SANDWICHES

4 servings

I usually make and chill the crabmeat filling for these sandwiches in the morning. Right before lunch, I fill the buns and heat them in the oven as we sail. 20 minutes later, we enjoy a delicious hot sandwich without stopping!

4 whole wheat sandwich buns or 8 slices whole wheat bread
1 can (7½ oz.) crabmeat, flaked
1 can (8 oz.) mushroom stems and pieces, drained
¼ c. mayonnaise
¼ c. (2 oz.) freshly grated parmesan cheese
1 Tbsp. parsley flakes
1 tsp. lemon juice
¼ tsp. rosemary, crumbled
¼ tsp. thyme, crumbled
⅛ tsp. sage, crumbled
2 Tbsp. slivered almonds

1. Combine all ingredients except buns and almonds. Spread crabmeat mixture into each bun and top with almonds. Wrap in foil.
2. Bake at 350° for 20 minutes. Serve warm.

1 serving = 381 calories

SPICED ROAST BEEF SPREAD SANDWICHES

2 servings

1 can (4¾ oz.) roast beef spread
2 Tbsp. drained horseradish
½ Tbsp. Worcestershire sauce
1 Tbsp. parsley flakes
4 slices whole grain bread

In a small bowl, combine all ingredients and spread into 2 sandwiches.

1 serving = 326 calories

OPEN-FACED MUSHROOM AND CHEDDAR CHEESE SANDWICHES

4 servings

12 *mushrooms, sliced*
1 *small onion, chopped*
1 *Tbsp. liquid corn oil margarine or safflower oil*
4 *slices whole wheat bread*
1 *tomato, sliced*
4 *oz. cheddar cheese*
a dash of pepper

1. Sauté mushrooms and onion in margarine until soft.
2. Toast bread slices in broiler or in a frying pan, then top with a tomato slice, mushroom-onion mixture, a dash of pepper, and cheese.
3. Broil or heat sandwiches in a frying pan until cheese is melted. Eat with a knife and fork.

1 *serving* = 207 *calories*

HAM AND PINEAPPLE SANDWICHES

4 servings

8 *slices whole grain bread*
2 *cans (4½ oz. each) deviled ham spread*
1 *can (8¼ oz.) sliced pineapple, drained (or 4 slices fresh pineapple)*
1 *large green onion, sliced*

Spread 4 slices of bread with ham. Top each with a pineapple ring and sprinkle with onion, then top with remaining bread slices.

1 *serving* = 344 *calories*

VEGETARIAN POCKET SANDWICHES

4 servings

3 Tbsp. peanut butter
1 c. plain low-fat yogurt
2 c. shredded lettuce
1 medium tomato, coarsely chopped
1 medium cucumber, coarsely chopped
1 small onion, coarsely chopped
4 pocket breads (2 oz. each), 1 inch cut off each
1 c. alfalfa sprouts (for sprouting instructions, see pages 48–49)

1. In a small bowl, beat peanut butter and yogurt until well mixed.
2. In a large bowl, combine lettuce, tomato, cucumber and onion.
3. Fill each pocket bread with vegetable mixture, peanut-yogurt dressing and sprouts.

1 serving = 238 calories

PEANUT BUTTER– COTTAGE CHEESE– RAISIN SANDWICHES

4 servings

⅓ c. peanut butter
½ c. low-fat cottage cheese
¼ c. raisins
8 slices whole wheat bread

Combine peanut butter, cottage cheese and raisins and spread into 4 sandwiches.

1 serving = 305 calories

4

DINNER

Dinner afloat usually means the end of a sailing day and brings with it satisfaction and a sense of accomplishment. Sometimes, though, this accomplishment can leave you too tired to cook—you just want to sit still for a while, eat, and then curl up into your bunk with a good book. I sometimes make Pressure-Cooked Hamburger and Potato Dinner (page 91) at times like that, and it really tastes great. In this book I have provided plenty of quick and satisfying recipes for those low-energy times.

But there are also days when the sailing is much more relaxed. You spend a leisurely day with friends just cruising around the bay, chatting and enjoying the sunshine. As dinner time rolls around, you find that you still have a lot of energy and want to whip up an outstanding gourmet creation from your tiny galley! I recall one such occasion when friends of ours joined us for a day sail to Prudence Island. We anchored there and spent a few delightful hours talking and windsurfing. On the sail home I began cooking up my favorite gourmet meal—Chicken Marsala (page 86), Caesar Salad (page 115), Brown Rice Pilaf (page 99), and Meringue Bowls with Fresh Fruit (page 126) for dessert. (I had made the meringue bowls and salad dressing at home ahead of time.) I lit several candles in the main cabin, and everyone enjoyed the food and atmosphere.

Even if we don't have friends along, Rick and I sometimes like to have a special home-cooked gourmet meal just for ourselves. On a recent vacation cruise to Martha's Vineyard, we dropped anchor in Katama Bay, having earlier stopped in Edgartown to stock up on fresh provisions. That evening we treated ourselves to Chicken Diable (page 80), Brown Rice, and Broccoli with Lemon-Garlic Sauce (page 118). For dessert we had Dipping Strawberries (page 123). We were particularly glad to have dined aboard that night. It would have been a shame to miss the beautiful sunset in that secluded, shallow, sand-encircled bay.

Whether you choose the quick recipes in this chapter or the ones that are more ambitious, all are selected with your health in mind. The recipes built around meat, fish, and poultry call for small portions (3–4 ounces) to keep down the fat and cholesterol. And there are a variety of delicious vegetarian meals included as well.

So, light the oil lamps and candles and enjoy your dinner!

MEALS WITH MEAT

To our normal way of looking at things, dinners are built around meat (or fish or poultry), with vegetables and grains as side dishes. When someone asks, "What's for dinner?" our usual response is something like "Baked chicken," "Tuna casserole," or "Pepper steak." The meat is the featured item.

It's hard for even a nutritionist to challenge such deeply engrained habits. But for the record, it's worth noting that one of the most significant ways to begin to lower our cholesterol level—and with it, our risk of heart attack—is by cutting down on animal food intake. Instead of planning our meals around meats, we should be doing exactly the opposite: using meats as condiments and flavor enhancers and planning our main courses around grains, legumes (dried peas, beans, and lentils), and vegetables. For sailors, there are particularly strong reasons for learning to rely more heavily on legumes as cooking staples. In addition to being good protein sources with none of the cholesterol found in animal foods, they are also inexpensive and easy to store.

When you do feature meat as the main course, here are some things you can do to keep the cholesterol down:

• Buy lean meats and trim off excess fat. With poultry, remove the skin before cooking.

• Reduce the size of your meat portions. Most nutrition tables list the cholesterol counts of meats based on a 3-ounce serving—or in other words, a portion of cooked meat about the size of a 3-inch hamburger, ½ inch thick. A restaurant portion of steak could easily be 12 ounces or more: four times the serving size, and four times the cholesterol.

• Be aware as well that there is no such thing as no-cholesterol animal food. Many people are under the impression that they can eat all the chicken they want without having to worry about cholesterol. In fact, however, the cholesterol content of chicken (74 mg per 3-ounce serving) is not significantly lower than that of lean meat (77 mg). Fish and shellfish are somewhat lower (in the 30–65 range), but again, large portions can quickly offset these reductions. When considering cholesterol from animal fats, it's not only *what* you eat, but *how much*.

A Word About Saturated Fat

Reducing cholesterol is an important step toward nutritional health. But for this step to be really effective, you need to be aware of saturated fat as well. If a food is high in saturated fat, it raises blood cholesterol, even if it contains little or no cholesterol itself. All animal foods (including dairy products such as eggs, whole milk, and butter) contain saturated fat, but it is also found in certain vegetable oils commonly used in cooking. Coconut oil and palm oil are highly saturated, as are hydrogenated fats such as shortening and many margarines.

This means that the way we prepare our meals has a lot to do with how healthy they are. Here are some suggestions for more healthful cooking:

• Bake, broil, or pan-broil rather than fry. (Pan-broiling means cooking meat or poultry without fat in a covered, heavy pan on low heat, turning food once or twice. After food is cooked, turn up heat to brown, then drain off excess fat.)

• Use vegetable oils that are low in saturated fats. Safflower oil is highest in polyunsaturated fat and is a healthier choice than ordinary vegetable oil or solid shortening, both of which contain saturated fat. Sunflower oil, corn oil, and soybean oil are also excellent choices; all of these polyunsaturated oils actually *lower* blood cholesterol. Recent research has indicated that olive oil and peanut oil also have a beneficial effect in lowering cholesterol.

When buying margarine, look for a label listing liquid corn oil, safflower oil, or sunflower oil as the first ingredient. Margarine in tub form is preferable to stick margarine as it contains less saturated fat. Either is better for you (and cheaper) than butter, which is high in cholesterol.

Incidentally, one of the worst culprits for saturated fats is nondairy creamer. This is a real junk food, high in hydrogenated fats, preservatives, and artificial flavoring and coloring. Better to learn to drink coffee black or with nonfat dry milk if you're out of fresh milk.

• Don't be afraid to reduce the amount of cooking oil or margarine called for in recipes—in most cases you can do so without noticing any change in flavor. If a recipe calls for 4 Tbsp. of margarine to sauté, use 1 Tbsp., or just enough to coat the pan. In all of the recipes in this cookbook I have tried to reduce fat content to the minimum.

• Make your own pastries rather than relying on store-bought ones, which are often high in saturated fats. The pastry label may state "vegetable oil," but this could be coconut or palm oil, and usually is. Boxed muffin and cake mixes contain similar saturated fats, so I don't recommend them.

• Use nonstick pans that require no greasing, or use a nonstick spray made from a vegetable oil low in saturated fat.

• Drain grease from hamburger before adding it to casseroles. Skim the fat off the tops of soups or stews before serving.

RECIPE SUBSTITUTIONS TO MAKE RECIPES HEALTHIER

This chart may be used as a guide for adapting your recipes to make them lower in fat, saturated fat and cholesterol. I find that many of the substitutions are actually more convenient for boat stowage. For example, I always have oil on the boat, but may not have butter. Evaporated skim milk is easier to keep than light cream, and nonfat dry milk is easier to keep than whole milk.

For This Food	Substitute This
1 whole egg	2 egg whites *or* 1 egg white and 1 tsp. safflower oil
1 egg yolk	1 egg white
1 c. whole milk	1 c. skim milk
1 c. buttermilk	2 c. skim milk plus 1 tsp. lemon juice or vinegar
1 c. butter	⅞ c. oil *or* 1 c. liquid corn oil margarine
1 c. shortening or lard	1 c. oil *or* 1 c. oil plus 3 Tbsp. liquid corn oil margarine
1 c. light cream	1 c. evaporated skim milk
1 c. sour cream	1 c. plain, low-fat yogurt
1 oz. (1 square) baking chocolate	3 Tbsp. powdered cocoa plus 1 Tbsp. oil
1 c. thin white sauce	1 Tbsp. oil, 1 Tbsp. flour, 1 c. skim milk, ¼ tsp. salt, dash of white pepper
1 c. medium white sauce	2 Tbsp. oil, 2 Tbsp. flour, 1 c. skim milk, ¼ tsp. salt, dash of white pepper
1 c. thick white sauce	3 Tbsp. oil, 4 Tbsp. flour, 1 c. skim milk, ¼ tsp. salt, dash of white pepper

SKILLET CHICKEN MOZZARELLA

4 servings

Traditionally, chicken is batter-coated and fried in oil or butter before being topped with sauce and cheese. In this recipe, I have omitted that step, yet the flavor is still the same. Therefore, time and needless fat calories are saved. This is a relatively quick meal to prepare and is just great with salad, garlic bread, and broiled peaches for a garnish (recipe follows).

1 *medium green pepper*
1 *small onion*
2 *medium zucchini*
2 *large chicken breasts, boned, skinned and split*
1 *c. spaghetti sauce*
¼ *tsp. salt (optional)*
⅛ *tsp. pepper*
½ *tsp. sugar*
¼ *c. sherry (optional)*
4 *oz. part-skim mozzarella cheese, sliced*

1. Cut green pepper into bite-sized pieces. Slice onion. Cut each zucchini lengthwise into quarters. Cut each quarter into ¾-inch chunks. Set vegetables aside.
2. Pound each chicken breast half into ¼-inch thickness with a mallet.
3. Spray a large skillet with a nonstick spray, or oil lightly. Cook chicken halves until lightly browned on both sides. Remove chicken to a plate.
4. Add more nonstick spray to pan and cook onion and green pepper until tender-crisp, stirring frequently. (Add a little water to prevent sticking if necessary.)
5. Return chicken to skillet and add spaghetti sauce, salt, pepper, sugar, sherry and zucchini. Over medium heat, heat to boiling. Reduce heat to low; cover and simmer for 15 minutes or until chicken and vegetables are fork-tender.
6. Top chicken breasts with mozzarella cheese; cover and simmer for about 2 minutes or until cheese is melted, then serve.

1 *serving* = 346 *calories*

BROILED PEACHES

4 servings

4 canned peach halves
2 tsp. raspberry, strawberry or grape jelly or jam (for color)

1. Place peach halves in a small baking dish and fill each peach center with ½ tsp. jelly.
2. Broil until lightly browned, then serve as a lovely garnish.

1 serving = 50 calories

10-MINUTE GOURMET CHICKEN

2 servings

Try this recipe when you're rushed for time yet want a really special candlelight dinner on your boat! I use yogurt instead of heavy cream in the sauce. Serve with salad and Brown Rice Pilaf (page 99), and don't forget the wine!

1 large chicken breast, skinned, boned and split
1 Tbsp. liquid corn oil margarine
1 large sweet apple, peeled, cored and sliced into circles or thin wedges
1 medium zucchini, grated
salt and pepper to taste
1 tsp. tarragon
several splashes of cognac
1 Tbsp. flour
½ c. plain low-fat yogurt

1. Flatten chicken breasts with a mallet.
2. Heat margarine in a large frying pan on high heat. Add chicken, apple slices, zucchini, salt, pepper and tarragon. When both sides of the chicken are lightly browned, splash with cognac and flambé.

3. Remove chicken, apple slices and zucchini to a serving platter or individual plates.
4. Add flour to pan drippings and splash with more cognac. Cook and stir mixture for a minute, then flambé again. Add yogurt and heat for another minute, but don't let the mixture boil. Pour the sauce over the chicken and serve.

1 serving = 310 calories

CHICKEN DIABLE

6 servings

This delightfully sweet chicken recipe is very easy to prepare but does take an hour to bake. It's a good recipe for when you and your guests plan on relaxing in the cockpit before dinner. While it's baking, cook up some brown rice and make a salad or green vegetable to go with it. If you'd like extra sauce to go on the rice, simply double the sauce recipe.

I once made this recipe for guests who sailed with us to Block Island. We arrived early enough so I had plenty of time to prepare the chicken. While it baked, we enjoyed the most incredible July sunset I have ever seen—with vibrant stripes of pink, blue and purple coloring the sky.

4 large chicken breasts, skinned, boned and split
2 Tbsp. safflower oil
½ c. honey
¼ c. prepared mustard
½ tsp. salt
1 tsp. curry powder

1. Cut each split chicken breast in half and arrange in a lightly oiled or nonstick-sprayed shallow baking dish.
2. Combine remaining ingredients and pour over chicken.
3. Bake at 375° for 1 hour.

1 serving = 340 calories following above recipe
479 calories with double sauce

STIR-FRIED CHICKEN WITH NUTS

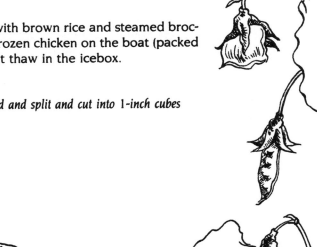

6 servings

This quick and spicy dish goes well with brown rice and steamed broccoli with lemon juice. I usually take frozen chicken on the boat (packed in a Tupperware container) and let it thaw in the icebox.

4 *large chicken breasts, boned, skinned and split and cut into 1-inch cubes*
1 *Tbsp. cornstarch*
2 *Tbsp. water*
1 *Tbsp. soy sauce*
2 *Tbsp. safflower oil*
2 *tsp. ground ginger*
2 *cloves garlic, minced*
¼ *tsp. crushed red pepper flakes*

SAUCE

2 *tsp. sugar*
2 *tsp. cornstarch*
4 *Tbsp. soy sauce*
2 *Tbsp. water*
2 *Tbsp. dry sherry*
2 *tsp. vinegar*
1 *tsp. sesame, peanut or safflower oil*
½ *c. peanuts or walnuts*
½ *lb. pea pods*

1. Combine chicken cubes with mixture of cornstarch, water and soy sauce.
2. Heat a wok or frying pan until very hot; add oil. Quickly stir-fry chicken in oil until done. Remove to a separate dish.
3. Add ginger, garlic, and red pepper to wok.
4. Combine sauce ingredients in a cup. Return chicken to wok and pour in the sauce, stirring until it thickens.
5. Stir in peanuts or walnuts and pea pods, then serve.

1 *serving* = 361 *calories*

WONDERFUL CHICKEN CURRY

6 servings

I first tried chicken curry while visiting my cousin in St. Croix before a charter sail in the British Virgin Islands. To my delight, the waiter wheeled out an enormous cart full of toppings for the curry! You'll find this to be a very pleasing company dish when served with a salad, brown rice, and as many toppings as you care to present.

Since the curry takes a while to cook, I usually make it ahead of time, store it in a Tupperware container and place it in the freezer at home. I then take the frozen curry to the boat and let it thaw in the icebox. When I'm ready to use it, all I have to do is heat and serve.

4 Tbsp. liquid corn oil margarine
2½ c. chopped onions
2 cloves garlic, chopped
½–1 tsp. salt
1 pod cardamom
2 Tbsp. curry powder
¼ tsp. black pepper
1 cinnamon stick
4 large chicken breasts, skinned, boned and split
1 tomato, diced
3 c. hot water
3 Tbsp. cornstarch

1. In a large pot, melt margarine and cook onions and garlic in the margarine until soft.
2. Add seasonings and stir, then add chicken and tomato and cook until the chicken is light brown.
3. Add 3 c. hot water and simmer until the chicken is tender and the sauce is reduced to half (about 1 hour). Break the chicken up into small pieces as it cooks.
4. Mix the cornstarch with a little water in a small cup and add to the chicken curry. Heat until the sauce thickens and comes to a boil. Serve hot on brown rice with any toppings listed opposite.

1 serving = 326 calories (not including rice or toppings)

TOPPING SUGGESTIONS

Sweet chutney
Unsalted peanuts
Chopped scallions
Raisins
Sesame seeds
Chopped green or red peppers
Chopped dried apricots

CHICKEN DIJON

4 servings

I replaced heavy cream with yogurt in this traditional recipe to make it more healthy with less saturated fat. You'll find that it tastes just as great, and you'll also save plenty of calories. The tangy flavor of this dish goes well with a sweet vegetable or fruit salad.

2 large chicken breasts, skinned and boned
1 Tbsp. liquid corn oil margarine
2 Tbsp. flour
½ c. chicken broth
½ c. white wine
½ c. plain low-fat yogurt
2 Tbsp. Dijon mustard

1. Cut chicken breasts into halves and pound with a mallet to ½-inch thickness.
2. Sauté chicken in a large skillet in margarine for 20 minutes. Set aside on a platter.
3. Stir flour into pan drippings, then add broth and wine. Cook and stir until mixture thickens and bubbles. Add a few spoonfuls of this sauce to the yogurt in a small cup (to warm it), then add the yogurt to the sauce in the pan. Add the mustard and chicken and heat through for 10 minutes but do not boil, as boiling will cause the yogurt to separate.
4. Serve with brown rice and Cinnamon-Glazed Carrots (recipe follows).

1 serving = 208 calories

CINNAMON-GLAZED CARROTS

4 servings

1 lb. bag carrots
½ c. water
1 Tbsp. liquid corn oil margarine
¼ tsp. salt
¼ tsp. cinnamon
1 Tbsp. honey
1 tsp. lemon juice
¼ c. chopped walnuts (optional)

1. Cut carrots into 3-inch strips. Place in a large skillet and add water, margarine and salt. Cover and cook until tender-crisp, about 5 to 10 minutes, adding a little more water if necessary. When carrots are tender, liquid should be nearly gone.
2. Gently stir in cinnamon, honey, and lemon juice and simmer for a few minutes. Add walnuts if desired and heat 1 minute longer.

1 serving = 126 calories with walnuts
79 calories without walnuts

HIBACHI PEANUT CHICKEN OR PORK KABOBS

4 servings

This unusual marinade may be used for chicken or pork. It's very flavorful as is, but if you like your food very spicy you can double the marinade recipe and reserve half to use as a dipping sauce. Serve with brown rice and a salad.

2 *Tbsp. peanut butter*
1 *Tbsp. brown sugar*
2 *Tbsp. lime or lemon juice*
¼ *c. soy sauce*
1 *clove garlic, finely chopped*
1 *tsp. finely chopped gingerroot*
½ *tsp. crushed red pepper*
1 *lb. boneless chicken and/or pork, cut into 1-inch cubes*
2 *green peppers, cut into 1-inch squares*

1. Combine first seven ingredients and mix well. Add chicken and/or pork and stir. Cover and chill in the icebox for 4 hours or overnight.
2. Thread chicken and/or pork and green pepper squares onto 4 large or 8 small skewers.
3. Grill over hot coals for 10 to 15 minutes, or until browned and cooked through, turning twice.

1 serving = 231 *calories with chicken*
            291 *calories with pork*

CHICKEN MARSALA

6 servings

This recipe requires more preparation time than most recipes, but there are some sailors (myself included) who occasionally enjoy going all out for a special gourmet meal. Serve this dish with Caesar Salad (page 115), Brown Rice Pilaf (page 99), and Broiled Peaches (page 79) for a really great presentation!

3 large chicken breasts, skinned, boned and split
1 egg, beaten with a fork
¼ c. skim milk
½ c. flour
1 tsp. salt
¼ tsp. pepper
1 Tbsp. olive oil
1 Tbsp. liquid corn oil margarine
1 small green pepper, cut into ¼-inch x 1½-inch strips
1 small onion, chopped
½ lb. mushrooms, sliced
1 clove garlic, minced
2 c. Marsala wine
2 envelopes instant chicken broth
1 Tbsp. cornstarch
1 lemon, cut into 6 thin slices

1. Pound chicken pieces to ¼-inch thickness with a wooden mallet.
2. Combine egg and milk in a shallow dish. Combine flour, salt and pepper on waxed paper. Dip chicken pieces into egg mixture, then into flour mixture, to coat all sides. Chill in the icebox between pieces of waxed paper for 2 hours.
3. Heat oil and margarine in a large skillet. Brown chicken pieces on both sides. Remove to a platter.
4. Sauté green pepper, onion, mushrooms, and garlic in the skillet until they are barely tender. Remove to a platter.
5. Add wine, chicken broth, and cornstarch mixed in a little water to the skillet. Boil, uncovered, for about 5 minutes or until the sauce has thickened.
6. Return chicken and vegetables to the skillet and heat thoroughly. Arrange chicken, vegetables, and sauce on a serving platter or on individual plates; top with lemon slices and serve.

1 serving = 290 calories

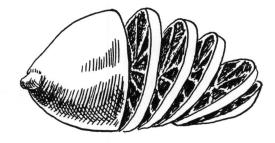

SALMON LOAF
WITH DILL SAUCE

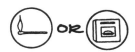

6 servings

Recently, researchers have found evidence that oily fish, particularly salmon, mackerel, sardines, and menhaden, contain beneficial fatty acids which reduce blood cholesterol and may have an anticancer potential as well. This recipe provides a great way to get some fish oils into your diet, and the ingredients are easily stowed. If you don't have an oven, or want to speed things up, you can fry salmon patties instead.

1 *can (15 oz.) salmon, drained and with any visible bones removed*
1 *small onion, chopped*
2 *eggs*
1 *tsp. parsley flakes*
1 *c. bread crumbs*
1 *large stalk celery, chopped*
¼ *tsp. pepper*

1. In a medium-sized bowl, combine all ingredients and mix well. Add a few Tbsp. water if the mixture looks dry.
2. Form into a loaf and place in a lightly oiled or nonstick-sprayed loaf pan.
3. Bake at 375° for 45 minutes or until brown. (Alternatively, form into patties and cook on a lightly oiled or nonstick-sprayed frying pan until brown.) Serve with Dill Sauce (recipe follows).

1 *serving* = 230 *calories*

DILL SAUCE

1 cup

2 Tbsp. safflower oil or liquid corn oil margarine
2 Tbsp. flour
1 c. skim milk
¼ tsp. salt
⅛ tsp. pepper
1 tsp. dill weed

1. In a small saucepan, heat oil or margarine over medium heat. Add flour, blend well and cook for several minutes until smooth and bubbly, stirring constantly.
2. Stir in milk, salt and pepper. Cook over medium heat for about 5 minutes, stirring constantly, until mixture comes to a boil and thickens. Serve warm.

1 Tbsp. = 24 calories

POOR MAN'S LOBSTER

4 servings

To me, this fish recipe tastes just like lobster! Serve with rice and steamed asparagus with Lemon-Garlic Sauce (page 118) for a delightful meal.

If it's convenient, I try to buy fresh fish while ashore at our cruising destination and use it right away. Or I buy it at home, transfer the fresh or frozen haddock into a Tupperware container, then freeze it until I transfer it to the boat, where I store it on the ice until ready to use. That way, I don't have to get rid of any smelly fish wrappers and the icebox doesn't get fishy.

1 lb. haddock (fresh or frozen)
water to cover
3 Tbsp. lemon juice (1½ lemons)
2 Tbsp. liquid corn oil margarine

DIPPING SAUCE

    3 Tbsp. lemon juice (1 ½ lemons)
    3 Tbsp. liquid corn oil margarine

1. Simmer haddock in water (just covering) with lemon juice and margarine for about 10 to 12 minutes if fresh, or 20 minutes if frozen, or until flaky.
2. Melt margarine and stir in lemon juice.
3. Serve fish with dipping sauce on the side.

1 serving = 221 calories

QUICK FISH CHOWDER

6 servings

This hearty chowder is high in protein and calcium and very low in fat. It's a great ending to a full day of sailing when you're tired and starved. Serve with Layered Tossed Salad (page 114) and whole grain bread.

   You can cook this ahead and freeze it for a really quick meal. The frozen chowder can sit on the ice in your icebox and thaw out while you sail.

    2 lb. haddock fillets, skinned and cut in pieces
    6 medium potatoes (2 lbs.), cut in chunks
    1 large onion, chopped
    1 can (13 oz.) evaporated skim milk
    3 c. skim milk
    1 Tbsp. liquid corn oil margarine
    Salt and pepper to taste

1. Simmer haddock in salted water (just enough to cover) for 10 minutes.
2. Add potatoes and onion and simmer for 20 minutes.
3. Add evaporated milk, skim milk, margarine, salt, and pepper. Simmer until heated through, then serve.

1 serving = 272 calories

ONE-SKILLET
BEEF-NOODLE MEDLEY

6 servings

I like to serve this quick and hearty dish with whole grain bread or muffins and fresh fruit. I usually take frozen ground beef to the boat in a Tupperware container and let it sit on the ice in the icebox and thaw while we sail.

> 1 lb. lean ground beef
> 1 medium onion, chopped
> 1 can (8 oz.) whole kernel corn
> 1 can (8 oz.) tomato sauce
> 2 c. (4 oz.) uncooked noodles
> 2 c. water
> 1 tsp. oregano, crumbled
> ½ tsp. salt
> ¼ tsp. pepper
> 1 Tbsp. parsley flakes
> 4 oz. (1 c.) cheddar cheese, shredded

1. Cook and stir meat and onion in a large skillet until meat is browned. Drain grease. Add all remaining ingredients except cheese.
2. Heat mixture to boiling. Lower heat; simmer uncovered, stirring occasionally, for 20 minutes or until noodles are tender. Stir in cheese and heat for a few minutes until cheese melts, then serve.

1 serving = 322 calories

STEAKS AU POIVRE PAVILLON

4 servings

If you are trying to learn to cook without salt, try this wonderful recipe from *Craig Claiborne's Gourmet Diet* (New York: Times Books, 1980). You won't miss salt at all if you substitute appropriate spices, herbs and seasonings as outlined on the next page.

4 boneless shell steaks, 4 ounces per person
1 tsp. black peppercorns
1 Tbsp. peanut, vegetable, or corn oil
¼ c. finely chopped shallots
2 Tbsp. cognac
½ c. dry red wine
2 Tbsp. unsalted butter or margarine
2 Tbsp. finely chopped parsley

1. Put the peppercorns on a flat surface and, using the bottom of a heavy skillet, crush them until they are coarse-fine.
2. Dip the steaks on both sides in the peppercorns, pressing the pepper into the meat.
3. Heat the oil in a large, heavy skillet and add the steaks. Cook over moderately high heat until the steaks are seared on one side, about 5 minutes. Turn and cook on the other side until seared, about 3 minutes.
4. Transfer the steaks to a warm serving dish. Pour off the fat from the skillet. Add the shallots and cook briefly, stirring. Add the cognac and stir; then add the wine and cook down for about 1 minute. Remove the skillet from the heat and swirl in the butter or margarine. Pour the sauce over the meat. Sprinkle with parsley and serve.

1 serving = 275 calories

PRESSURE-COOKED HAMBURGER AND POTATO DINNER

6 servings

This meal can be prepared quickly and is high in protein and vitamin C. It's very satisfying when you're starving after a long sail. Serve with Carrot-Raisin Salad (page 113) and a green vegetable.

I remember making this dish for our very first cruising meal. We had a 25-foot sloop and had sailed to a small cove in Narragansett Bay. I was exhilarated by the surroundings, and found cooking to be great fun out in the fresh air with the cabin hatch open.

1 lb. lean ground beef
1 medium onion, diced
2 large stalks celery, diced
7 medium potatoes, sliced thin
½ tsp. salt
1 can (16 oz.) tomatoes
¼ c. water

1. Brown ground beef, onion, and celery in a pressure cooker. Drain grease.
2. Add the remaining ingredients.
3. Cover, set control at 15 pounds pressure and cook for 3 minutes after the control knob jiggles. (Reduce heat so that control jiggles only 1 to 3 times per minute.)
3. Reduce pressure instantly by dipping the cooker in a bucket of sea-water, then serve.

1 serving = 275 calories

PICADILLO

8 servings

This was one of Ernest Hemingway's favorite recipes. It's quick and easy and tastes great over brown rice with Creamy Cucumbers on the side (recipe follows).

2 c. raisins
½ c. hot beef broth
2 lbs. lean ground beef
2 c. red wine
¾ c. finely chopped green onions with tops
1 tsp. salt
2 cloves garlic, minced
½ tsp. oregano
¼ tsp. ground cloves
¼ tsp. black pepper
2 green peppers, chopped
¾ c. slivered almonds
brown rice, cooked

1. Soak raisins in broth for 10 minutes or until plump; drain and set aside.
2. Brown beef in a large skillet for 3 to 5 minutes; drain grease.
3. Add the wine, onions, salt, garlic, oregano, cloves, and pepper. Simmer 15 minutes. Stir in green peppers and cook 5 minutes longer. Stir in almonds and raisins. If the mixture is too wet, add 1 Tbsp. cornstarch mixed in a little water to thicken. Serve hot over brown rice.

1 serving = 414 calories

CREAMY CUCUMBERS

4 servings

In this recipe, yogurt replaces sour cream to decrease the fat and calories.

3 large cucumbers
1 tsp. salt
1 Tbsp. sugar
½ tsp. salt
½ tsp. dry mustard
3 Tbsp. vinegar
1 c. plain low-fat yogurt
½ tsp. onion powder

1. Peel and thinly slice cucumbers and add 1 tsp. salt. Soak in ice water for 2 hours. Drain and press dry.
2. Add sugar, salt, dry mustard, vinegar, yogurt, and onion powder. Mix well, then serve.

1 serving = 55 calories

VEGETARIAN MEALS

Any sailor who embarks on long voyages or cruises in an area lacking frequent opportunity to restock food supplies can benefit from learning to rely more heavily on vegetarian cooking. The staples required—dried beans and peas, whole grains, whole grain flour and pasta, nuts and seeds—are inexpensive, fairly nonperishable, and easy to store. In addition, they provide you with high fiber in your diet and no cholesterol.

But is it really possible to get all the protein you need from vegetable sources? Yes— if you know how to combine them properly. Nine essential amino acids are needed for protein synthesis; animal foods contain all nine. Plant foods are short on one or more of these essential amino acids. For example, grains are limited in the amino acid lysine but are high in methionine. Legumes are low in methionine but high in lysine. When you combine grains and legumes—as, for example, in a bean and rice casserole (see page 104)—the essential amino acids work together to provide complete protein. Through judicious combination of plant proteins, you can easily equal or exceed the amount of protein available in a meat-based diet.

This process, known as protein complementation, is not difficult to master. Most of the combinations are so obvious that it's difficult to *avoid* them—as can be seen from a glance at the items on the accompanying chart. The addition of dairy products makes protein complementation even easier. (While it's true that eggs, whole milk, and cheese add cholesterol, the amount is usually less than in a meat-based meal, so long as you avoid rich egg-and-cream combinations.)

A word of caution, however. "Complete" protein merely means that the essential amino acids are all present so that protein synthesis can occur; it does *not* mean that a particular food contains your full daily allowance of protein. To be sure of getting enough protein, you need to plan your meals around a variety of these protein-complete combinations, using the recommended daily servings from each of the four food groups (see pages 6–14) as your guide. Here are sample menu plans for two days of nutritionally complete vegetarian cooking, using some of the recipes from this book:

Day 1

Breakfast
Peanut butter
Oatmeal–Oat Bran Muffins,   Grains/Legumes
    page 36
Orange juice
Cocoa
Lunch
Hummus, page 59   ⎫
Babaganouj, page 58   ⎬   Legumes/Seeds/Grains
Syrian bread triangles   ⎭
Carrot sticks
Fresh fruit salad
Dinner
Cheesy Beans and Rice,   ⎫
    page 104   ⎬   Dairy/Grains/Legumes
Cornbread, page 32   ⎭
Broccoli with Lemon-Garlic Sauce,
    page 118
Dipping Strawberries, page 123

Day 2

Breakfast
Banana Bran Pancakes,   Dairy/Grains
    page 30
Orange juice
Cocoa
Lunch
Crustless Spinach Pie,   ⎫
    page 54   ⎬   Dairy/Vegetables/Grains/
Chilled Sesame Linguine, ⎭   Legumes
    page 58
Fresh melon wedges
Dinner
Lentil Soup, page 62   ⎫
Whole Wheat Irish Soda Bread,   ⎬   Legumes/Grains
    page 38   ⎭
Carrot-Raisin Salad, 113
Vanilla Pudding, page 131
    sprinkled with Granola, page 27   Dairy/Grains

PROTEIN COMPLEMENTARY RELATIONSHIPS

The food combinations listed below take advantage of protein complementation to provide complete protein. Each item on the list contains all essential amino acids needed for protein synthesis.

Dairy Products or Eggs with Grains

Bread or rice pudding
Cereal and milk
Cheese fondue with bread
Cheese sandwich
Creamed soups with noodles or rice
Eggs and toast
Egg salad sandwich
Fettucine (pasta and cheese)

French toast
Macaroni and cheese
Meatless lasagna
Pancakes or waffles
Pizza
Quiche
Yogurt and crackers

Grains with Legumes

Baked beans and brown bread
Bean or lentil soup and bread
Bean and rice dishes
Corn tortillas or tacos and beans
Hummus (garbanzo bean paste)
    and bread

Lentils and rice
Peanut butter sandwich
Soybean sandwich
Split pea soup and cornbread
Tamale pie (beans and cornmeal)

Nuts and Seeds with Legumes

Bean soup with sesame seed muffins
Hummus with sesame seeds
Nuts and seeds snacks
Roasted soybeans and seed snacks
Tofu with sesame seeds

Other Vegetables with Dairy Products or Eggs

Bean-cheese salad
Cream of vegetable soup
Eggplant-artichoke parmesan
Escalloped potatoes
Potato salad with egg
Spinach or broccoli quiche
Spinach salad with eggs and cheese

HOW TO COOK BEANS

The one disadvantage of vegetarian cooking is that some of these foods, such as dried beans and peas, take a long time to cook. You can circumvent the problem by buying canned beans, but they take up a lot more storage space than dried beans. If you have the time, you're better off cooking your own; it's mostly just a matter of planning ahead. A pressure cooker, if you have one, helps speed the process along.

First, you need to soak your washed beans in a large pot with plenty of water covering them for at least 6 hours or overnight. If you forget to do this you can, instead, cover the beans with water, bring to a boil, simmer for 5 minutes, remove from the heat, and let sit for 1 hour. This is called a quick soak.

Regular Cooking Method

Beans (1 c. dry measure)	Water	Cooking Time
Black beans	4 cups	1½ hours
Black-eyed peas	3 cups	1 hour
Garbanzos (chick-peas)	4 cups	3 hours
Great northern beans	3½ cups	2 hours
Kidney beans	3 cups	1½ hours
Lentils	3 cups	1 hour
Limas	2 cups	1½ hours
Baby limas	2 cups	1½ hours
Navy beans	3 cups	1½ hours
Pinto beans	3 cups	2½ hours
Red beans	3 cups	3 hours
Soybeans	4 cups	3 hours or more
Soy grits (no need to soak)	2 cups	15 minutes
Split peas	3 cups	1 hour

Simply cover beans with water in a large pot, bring to a boil, reduce heat and simmer for the required amount of time, or until the beans are tender. Keep the pot partially covered at all times because it might boil over if covered tightly. If desired, add about ½ tsp. salt per cup of raw beans and any other seasonings you wish after the beans are tender. If the beans are done, the skins will shrink and crack away when you blow on them.

Pressure Cooker Method

Beans (1 c. dry measure)	Water	Cooking Time
Black beans	2 cups	30 minutes
Black-eyed peas	1½ cups	10 minutes
Garbanzos (chick-peas)	2 cups	35 minutes
Great northern beans	2 cups	20 minutes
Kidney beans	2 cups	30 minutes
Lentils	2 cups	20 minutes
Limas	2 cups	30 minutes
Baby limas	2 cups	25 minutes
Navy beans	2 cups	30 minutes
Pea beans	2 cups	20 minutes
Pinto beans	2 cups	10 minutes
Red beans	2 cups	35 minutes
Soybeans	2 cups	35 minutes
Split peas*	———	————

Place beans and water in a pressure cooker. Cover and bring to 15 pounds pressure, then reduce heat so that the control knob jiggles only 1 to 3 times per minute. After cooking time is up, reduce pressure by dipping pressure cooker into a pail of seawater. Season cooked beans as desired.

It's not recommended that you cook split peas in the pressure cooker because they tend to froth and sometimes block the vent tube.

Creative Cooking with Beans

Beans are great for the experimental cook because you can use your imagination on them and add anything you have on hand. Use them in soups, salads, and casseroles, and mash them up for sandwich fillings. Flavor them with herbs, hot pepper flakes, tomato sauce, soy sauce, vinegar, lemon juice, or vegetables. Just be sure to include grains, seeds, or dairy products for protein complementation. Combining them with cheese makes a really satisfying meal.

DINNER GRAINS

Whole grains are another basic staple of vegetarian cooking and are great for sailors because they are very easy to store and add a great deal of texture, flavor, and nutrition to meals. Like beans, they invite you to use your culinary imagination.

Besides brown rice, have you ever tried barley, bulgur, kasha (buckwheat groats), or browned oats for dinner? I enjoy the chewiness of barley and the totally unique flavor of kasha. Bulgur has a good, nutty flavor and may be used interchangeably in recipes with cracked wheat. Browned oats are quick and easy to make and are a good substitute for rice or pasta.

Simply by adding shredded cheese or legumes to any grains you will have a complete-protein meatless meal. For that reason, it's a good idea to keep a supply of grains and legumes on your boat as emergency rations in the event that you are unable to buy fresh provisions.

See pages 21–23 for instructions on cooking all types of grains. Here are several tasty recipes to try.

BROWN RICE PILAF

4 servings

Why buy the packaged mixes when you can easily make your own and get more fiber using brown rice?

    2 tsp. safflower oil
    1 small onion, chopped
    1 large stalk celery, chopped
    ½ c. brown rice
    ⅓ c. bulgur wheat
    2 c. beef broth (2 beef bouillon cubes dissolved in 2 c. boiling water)

1. In a large skillet, sauté onion, celery, brown rice, and bulgur in oil.
2. Add beef broth and bring to a boil.
3. Cover and simmer for 30 minutes, or until the rice and bulgur are tender and the broth is absorbed.

1 serving = 173 calories

BARLEY WITH DILL

8 servings

This recipe makes a delicious entree when cheddar cheese is added.

1¾ c. whole hulled barley
1 quart hot broth or bouillon
2 tsp. dill weed
1 (4 oz.) can mushrooms
2 onions, chopped
2 stalks celery, diced
2 Tbsp. safflower oil

1. In a large saucepan, bring the broth to a boil and slowly add the barley and stir. Add the dill, cover, and lower the heat. Cook for 25 to 30 minutes or until all of the broth has been absorbed.
2. In a pan, sauté the onions and celery in the oil. Add the mushrooms and heat through.
3. Add the vegetables to the cooked barley and serve.

1 serving = 205 calories

BROWNED OATS

4 servings

1½ c. oatmeal
1 egg, beaten with a fork
2 Tbsp. liquid corn oil margarine
¾ c. water, broth, or bouillon
¼ tsp. salt

1. Combine oats and egg, and mix until oats are thoroughly coated.
2. Melt margarine in a skillet and add oats mixture. Cook over medium heat, stirring constantly, for 3 to 5 minutes or until oats are dry, separated and lightly browned.

3. Add water and salt, continue cooking, stirring occasionally, for 2 to 3 minutes or until liquid evaporates, then serve.

1 serving = 175 calories

(*If desired, substitute orange juice for the water, or add ½ tsp. oregano, ½ tsp. basil, and 1 Tbsp. parsley.*)

TABOULI

6 servings

This refreshing dish is very high in vitamin A, beta-carotene, potassium, fiber and B vitamins. It can be made one or two days ahead of time and stored in a leakproof container in the icebox. To make this a complete protein meal, add 1 can (16 oz.) of drained chick-peas (garbanzo beans).

2 c. boiling water
1 c. bulgur or cracked wheat
1–2 c. fresh parsley, chopped
2 Tbsp. crumbled dry mint leaves (or ¼ c. chopped fresh)
1 onion, chopped
1 cucumber, diced
1 large carrot, shredded
3 Tbsp. lemon juice (1–2 lemons)
¼ c. olive oil
2 Tbsp. soy sauce
¼ tsp. black pepper
a pinch of garlic powder
lettuce leaves (optional)

1. In a large bowl, pour boiling water over bulgur and let stand for 1 hour or until light and fluffy. Drain off excess water.
2. Stir in parsley, mint leaves, onion, cucumber, and carrot.
3. In a small bowl, combine lemon juice, oil, soy sauce, pepper and garlic powder. Pour over bulgur mixture and blend well. Serve on a bed of lettuce, if desired.

1 serving = 189 calories

KASHA

6 servings

When you buy buckwheat groats for this recipe, make sure that they are chopped up and not whole. I once bought whole buckwheat by mistake and found that it didn't work in this recipe because it takes too long to cook—even using a pressure cooker.

    1 c. kasha (buckwheat groats)
    1 egg, beaten with a fork
    ½ tsp. salt
    ½ c. onion, finely chopped
    2½ c. boiling water
    1 Tbsp. liquid corn oil margarine
    4 Tbsp. chopped parsley

1. Combine the kasha and egg and cook over medium to low heat in a skillet, stirring occasionally, until the grains become separated. Be careful not to let burn.
2. Add remaining ingredients and stir. Bring to a boil, cover, and simmer for 25 minutes or until all of the liquid has been absorbed. Fluff with a fork and serve.

1 serving ▬ 124 calories

SOYBEAN CASSEROLE

6 servings   AND/OR

If you've never cooked soybeans before, go ahead and try them now! In this recipe, the soybeans resemble soft peanuts in flavor and texture. Soybeans are a great food value—inexpensive and high in protein. In fact, one serving of this recipe contains 35 grams of protein—the amount found in 5 ounces of meat. The cheese adds a lot of flavor and complements the amino acids in the beans. Also, the carrots give you plenty of vitamin A and beta-carotene!

1 lb. uncooked soybeans
4 c. water
1 lb. bag of carrots
4 large stalks celery
2 Tbsp. soy sauce
1 Tbsp. Worcestershire sauce
½ tsp. black pepper
several dashes onion and garlic powder
1 Tbsp. parsley flakes
1–2 shakes hot pepper flakes
8 oz. sharp cheddar cheese

1. Soak beans in a large pot overnight with plenty of water to cover, or cover beans with water, bring to a boil and let sit for 1 hour. (For more information on preparing beans, see page 97.)
2. Drain beans, add 4 c. water and simmer for ½ to 1 hour.
3. Add the remaining ingredients except cheese and simmer for another hour or until beans are done. (Beans are done when you can put a bean on your tongue and mash it against the roof of your mouth.)
4. Layer beans and cheese in a large casserole or individual casserole dishes with a layer of cheese on top. Bake at 300° for 20 to 30 minutes.

1 serving = 474 calories

Pressure Cooker Method

1. Follow step 1 as above, then combine all ingredients except cheese and place in a pressure cooker.

2. Pressure cook at 15 pounds pressure for 35 minutes. Let cooker cool for 5 minutes, then place in a bucket of seawater to release pressure.
3. Layer soybeans with cheese as in step 4 above and bake as indicated.

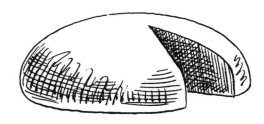

 **CHEESY BEANS AND RICE**

6 servings

To me, this is one of the world's most delightful dishes. Packed with protein, calcium, B vitamins and fiber, this meal will keep you full for hours. The beans and rice provide protein complementation and the cheese and cottage cheese supply additional protein. I like to serve it with cornbread and a fruit salad.

3 c. cooked brown rice (see page 22 for cooking instructions)
1 can (15½ oz.) kidney beans, drained
1 clove garlic, minced
1 large onion, chopped
1 can (4 oz.) chopped green chili peppers
4 oz. shredded cheese
1 c. low-fat cottage cheese
½ c. (2 oz.) grated sharp cheddar cheese

1. In a large bowl, combine rice, beans, garlic, onion, and chili peppers. Layer this mixture alternately with shredded cheese and cottage cheese in an oiled or nonstick-sprayed casserole dish. End with a layer of the bean-rice mixture.
2. Bake at 350° for 30 minutes. During the last few minutes of baking, sprinkle sharp cheddar cheese on top.

1 serving = 518 calories

TAMALE PIE
WITH OR WITHOUT CHEESE

6 servings

This satisfying vegetarian dish contains beans and cornmeal for protein complementation, plus nonfat dry milk powder for additional complete protein. It can be eaten with or without added cheese and is high in fiber, vitamins A and C, and calcium (when cheese is included).

1 Tbsp. safflower oil
1 large onion, chopped
1 medium green pepper, chopped
3½ c. chicken broth
1½ c. yellow cornmeal
½ c. nonfat dry milk powder
1 can (14½ oz.) tomatoes
1 can (12 oz.) corn, drained
1 can (15–20 oz.) red kidney beans (or 2 c. cooked beans)
1 Tbsp. chili powder
6 oz. Monterey Jack cheese (or cheese of your choice)

1. Heat oil in a large skillet over medium heat and add onion and green pepper. Cook until tender.
2. Meanwhile, in a medium-sized saucepan over medium heat, stir broth, cornmeal and milk powder for 5 to 10 minutes until smooth and thickened.
3. Add tomatoes (broken up with a fork), corn, kidney beans, and chili powder to onion and green pepper in skillet and stir. Reduce heat and simmer, uncovered, 15 minutes or until thickened.
4. Spread cornmeal mixture in the bottom and up the sides of an oiled or nonstick-sprayed 9-inch square or 12-inch x 7-inch baking pan. Pour in bean mixture.
5. Bake at 350° for about 45 minutes or until mixture is bubbly. Place cheese on top and return to oven until cheese melts.

1 serving = 402 calories with cheese
302 calories without cheese

EGGPLANT-ARTICHOKE PARMESAN CASSEROLE

4 servings

Traditionally, eggplant is deep-fried before being added to casseroles. In this recipe, time and calories are saved by baking the eggplant instead—with a small amount of mayonnaise or oil, and bread crumbs on top. The artichokes add a tangy, complementary taste. Serve with Spinach Salad (page 117) and garlic bread.

I remember making this in Tarpaulin Cove, Vineyard Sound, after a lazy sail over from Cape Cod. It was a warm, calm evening and we greatly enjoyed our sunset feast under our awning.

> 1 *medium-sized eggplant (1 lb.)*
> 1 *Tbsp. mayonnaise or oil*
> ¼ *c. bread crumbs*
> 1 *(6 oz.) jar artichoke hearts, well drained and cut into bite-sized pieces*
> 1 *Tbsp. lemon juice*
> 8 *oz. can tomato sauce with tomato bits*
> ½ *tsp. pepper*
> 1 *tsp. paprika*
> 1 *tsp. basil*
> ½ *tsp. garlic powder*
> 8 *oz. shredded part-skim mozzarella cheese*
> ¼ *c. freshly grated parmesan cheese*

1. Cut eggplant into ¼-inch thick crosswise slices and arrange in 1 layer on 2 lightly oiled or nonstick-sprayed cookie sheets. Spread each eggplant slice very lightly with the 1 Tbsp. mayonnaise or oil and bread crumbs. Bake at 475° for 15 minutes. Remove from oven and reduce oven temperature to 375°.
2. In a medium skillet, heat artichoke hearts and sprinkle with lemon juice. Add tomato sauce and seasonings.
3. In a lightly oiled or nonstick-sprayed baking dish, layer eggplant, artichoke mixture and mozzarella cheese. Make a second layer and top with parmesan cheese.
4. Bake at 375° for 15 to 20 minutes or until cheese is bubbly.

1 *serving* = 328 *calories*

ZUCCHINI LASAGNA

6 servings

This delicious lasagna is lower in calories than traditional lasagna because zucchini replaces pasta and low-fat cottage cheese replaces ricotta cheese. Serve with baked potatoes or whole grain bread and salad.

½ lb. lean ground beef
⅓ c. chopped onion
1 can (15 oz.) tomato sauce
½ tsp. salt
½ tsp oregano
¼ tsp. basil
⅛ tsp. pepper
4 medium zucchini
8 oz. low-fat cottage cheese
1 egg
2 Tbsp. flour
½ lb. part-skim mozzarella cheese, shredded

1. In a large skillet, over medium heat, cook ground beef and onion until onion is tender, about 10 minutes. Drain grease.
2. Add tomato sauce, salt, oregano, basil and pepper. Heat to boiling. Reduce heat to low and simmer for 5 minutes to blend flavors, stirring occasionally.
3. Slice zucchini lengthwise into ¼-inch thick slices.
4. In a small bowl, combine cottage cheese with egg until well mixed.
5. In the bottom of a large rectangular baking dish, arrange half of the zucchini in a layer and sprinkle with 1 Tbsp. of flour. Top with cottage cheese mixture and half of meat mixture. Repeat with remaining zucchini and flour; sprinkle with mozzarella and the remaining meat mixture.
6. Bake for 1 hour at 350° until hot and bubbly and zucchini is fork-tender. Let stand for 10 minutes before cutting.

1 serving = 283 calories

 AND

CREAMED CABBAGE
AND WALNUT CASSEROLE

4 servings

This quick, delicious vegetarian casserole is high in fiber, vitamin C, beta-carotene and calcium. I like to serve it with baked potatoes and steamed green beans, flavored with dill weed.

1 *medium cabbage, shredded*
¼ c. *liquid corn oil margarine*
2 *Tbsp. cornstarch*
½ *tsp. salt*
¼ *tsp. pepper*
2 c. *skim milk*
½ c. *chopped walnuts*
1 c. *(4 oz.) shredded cheese*
2 *Tbsp. bread crumbs*

1. Cook cabbage in a minimal amount of water (with or without salt) until tender.
2. Meanwhile, melt margarine in a saucepan over medium heat. Remove from heat and blend in cornstarch, salt and pepper. Gradually blend in milk. Cook over medium heat, stirring constantly, until mixture thickens and comes to a boil.
3. Drain cabbage well. In an oiled or nonstick-sprayed 1½-quart casserole dish, arrange alternate layers of cabbage, walnuts, sauce and cheese. Sprinkle with bread crumbs.
4. Bake at 450° for 10 minutes or until heated through and crumbs are lightly browned.

1 *serving* = 388 *calories*

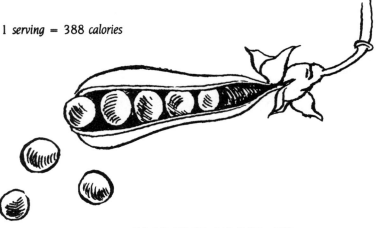

PASTA PRIMAVERA

6 servings

This colorful dish is high in vitamins A and C, B vitamins, beta-carotene, fiber, and calcium. If you can't find all of the ingredients, just improvise! Get a friend to help you chop the vegetables and then enjoy this dish with salad and fresh whole grain bread.

1 *bunch broccoli (about 1 lb.)*
2 *small zucchini*
½ *lb. asparagus*
1 *lb. linguine*
1 *large clove garlic, chopped*
1 *basket cherry tomatoes, halved*
2 *Tbsp. olive oil*
1 *tsp. basil, crumbled*
½ *lb. mushrooms, thinly sliced*
½ *c. frozen or fresh green peas*
2 *Tbsp. parsley flakes*
1 *tsp. salt*
¼ *tsp. black pepper*
¼ *tsp. crushed red pepper flakes*
2 *Tbsp. liquid corn oil margarine (or oil)*
1 *c. plain low-fat yogurt*
6 *oz. freshly grated parmesan cheese*

1. Wash and trim broccoli, zucchini and asparagus. Cut broccoli into bite-sized pieces; cut zucchini into thin slices; cut asparagus into 1-inch pieces. Steam or cook in a small amount of boiling water until tender-crisp; drain; put in a large bowl.
2. Cook and drain linguine.
3. Sauté garlic and tomatoes in oil in a large pot for 2 minutes. Stir in basil and mushrooms; cook for 3 minutes. Stir in peas, parsley, salt, and black and red pepper; cook 1 minute more. Add mixture to vegetables in bowl.
4. Melt margarine in same pot. Stir in yogurt and heat gently but do not boil. Add linguine and toss to coat. Add parmesan cheese and vegetables and toss well. Heat gently just until hot, then serve.

1 *serving* = 553 *calories*

INSTANT FETTUCINE

4 servings

You won't believe how easy and satisfying this meal is. It's great plain or with broccoli added, and it's much lower in fat than traditional fettucine with heavy cream. Serve with salad and tomatoes broiled with a little basil, garlic powder, parsley, pepper, parmesan cheese, and bread crumbs.

I use this recipe often on Sunday evenings when I want to serve a quick but delicious supper on the boat before we head home.

8 oz. dry whole wheat spaghetti or fettucine
5 oz. freshly grated parmesan cheese
1 Tbsp. liquid corn oil margarine or safflower oil
a dash of garlic powder
salt and freshly ground black pepper to taste

Cook spaghetti to desired doneness and drain. Toss with margarine and add garlic powder, salt, pepper, and parmesan cheese. Mix well and serve immediately. (Cheese will melt and get stringy as you mix it.)

1 serving = 350 calories

INSTANT FETTUCINE
WITH BROCCOLI

4 servings

1. Break a 1-pound head of broccoli into small florets and slice stalks into thin diagonal slices. Steam lightly until tender-crisp.
2. Add broccoli to the above recipe, mix well and serve immediately.

1 serving = 378 calories

CHEESE FONDUE

6 servings

Fondue is a festive food to serve a group on your boat, with bread and various fruits and raw vegetables for dipping. I prefer French bread for dipping, but you may like whole wheat bread just as well. Be sure to use a nonstick spray on your fondue pot to make cleaning easier. I've served this many times to guests on our boat. It's very quick and easy to prepare, and people really enjoy eating it.

> 1 *lb. Swiss cheese*
> ¼ *c. flour*
> 2 *c. white wine*
> 3 *oz. Kirschwasser liqueur*
> 3 *dashes nutmeg*
> *Salt and pepper to taste*

1. Cut cheese into 1-inch chunks and coat with flour.
2. Heat wine and add cheese. When cheese is melted, stir in the Kirschwasser, nutmeg, salt and pepper. Serve in a fondue pot over an alcohol or Sterno burner, with dipping forks and various dipping foods. If you don't have a fondue pot, you can use the pan that you cooked it in—but you'll have to eat fast because the cheese hardens as it cools!

1 serving = 320 calories

DIPPING SUGGESTIONS

French or whole wheat bread, cut in chunks
apple slices
pear slices
green pepper squares
mushroom halves
broccoli florets

 AND

BAKED ZITI
WITH THREE CHEESES

4 servings

This quick recipe goes well with whole grain bread and steamed broccoli with Tahini-Yogurt-Lemon Sauce (page 118).

> 2 c. meatless spaghetti sauce
> 8 oz. dry ziti (or other large-cut tubular pasta), cooked and well drained
> 2 c. low-fat cottage cheese
> 4 oz. shredded part-skim mozzarella cheese
> ½ c. (2 oz.) freshly grated parmesan cheese

1. In a 9-inch square baking dish, spread a thin layer of tomato sauce. Top with ¼ of the pasta, a thin layer of tomato sauce, and dollops of ¼ of the cottage cheese. Sprinkle with ¼ of the mozzarella cheese and 1 Tbsp. parmesan cheese. Repeat layers, ending with sauce and cheeses.
2. Bake at 400° for 20 minutes or until sauce is bubbly, cheese is melted, and top is lightly browned. Serve hot.

1 serving = 510 calories

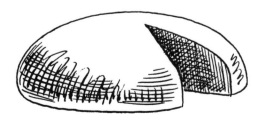

CARROT-RAISIN SALAD

6 servings

This wonderful, chewy salad is very high in vitamin A and beta-carotene. You can vary the recipe by adding nuts, seeds, or other fruits, and you can also eat it as a main dish if you add cheese to it (recipe follows).

2 lb. carrots, grated
¾ c. raisins
1 Tbsp. lemon juice
½ c. mayonnaise or plain low-fat yogurt

Combine all ingredients and serve on a bed of lettuce.

1 *serving* = 246 *calories with mayonnaise*
121 *calories with yogurt (recipe will be wetter)*

CARROT-RAISIN SALAD WITH CHEESE

6 servings

Follow the above recipe but add 9 ounces of your favorite cheese, cut into bite-sized cubes. Serve on a bed of lettuce.

1 *serving* = 396 *calories with mayonnaise*
271 *calories with yogurt*

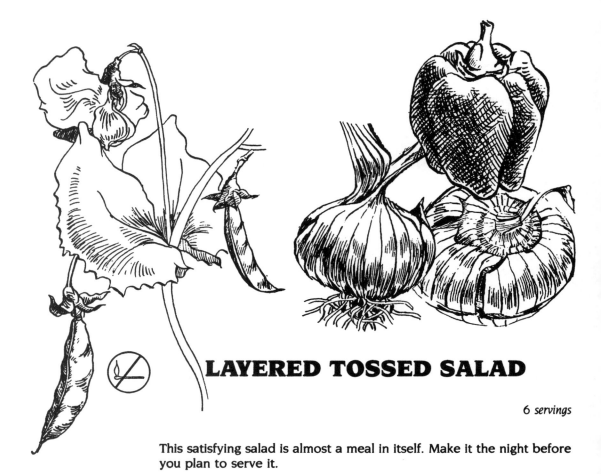

LAYERED TOSSED SALAD

6 servings

This satisfying salad is almost a meal in itself. Make it the night before you plan to serve it.

1 *head lettuce, broken into bite-sized pieces*
½ *c. chopped red and green onions*
½ *c. chopped celery*
½ *c. chopped green pepper*
1 *(10 oz.) pkg. frozen peas (or use fresh)*
1 *c. mayonnaise-type salad dressing*
2 *Tbsp. sugar*
½ *c. imitation bacon bits*
6 *oz. shredded cheddar cheese*

1. Layer all ingredients in a large salad bowl in the order given. (Don't cook the peas; add the salad dressing in spoonfuls.)
2. Let sit overnight. Toss just before serving.

1 serving = 342 calories

CAESAR SALAD

6 servings

My reduced-fat version of this traditional recipe could be a great addition to your favorite gourmet meal. I prefer to leave out the anchovies, but you may like them. Some people like to add a little anchovy paste to the dressing, too.

I usually make the croutons and dressing at home and transport them to the boat. Then all I have to do is wash the lettuce, add the egg and cheese, and toss with the dressing.

1 clove garlic, crushed
¼ c. olive oil
3 slices firm bread
3 Tbsp. fresh lemon juice (1½ lemons)
6 anchovy fillets, minced (optional)
¼ tsp. salt
½ tsp. dry mustard
⅛ tsp. coarse black pepper
½ tsp. Worcestershire sauce
1 egg
1 large head romaine lettuce
½ c. (2 oz.) freshly grated parmesan cheese

1. Steep garlic in oil overnight; remove the garlic and discard it. Cut bread into small cubes.
2. In a large skillet, sauté bread cubes in ¼ of the garlic oil until golden brown. Set aside.
3. Heat egg in hot water in a small bowl for 10 minutes while preparing dressing.
4. Combine remaining oil, lemon juice, anchovies, salt, mustard, pepper, and Worcestershire sauce in a large salad bowl.
5. Shred bite-sized pieces of romaine into salad bowl. Top romaine with half the parmesan. Break egg over salad. Toss salad, spooning from bottom of bowl, until greens are coated with dressing. Sprinkle with remaining parmesan and the sautéed bread. Serve at once.

1 *serving* = 185 *calories*

SUMMER PASTA SALAD

5 servings

This makes a great cold main dish and can be made up to a day ahead of the time you plan to serve it. It's high in protein, fiber, calcium and vitamin A and is quite filling.

I usually make it ahead of time for dinner on a day we plan to sail all day and I know I won't feel like cooking when we get to our destination. I also make it ahead for lunch so we can eat it while we sail and I won't have to spend time in the galley.

⅓ c. safflower oil
3 Tbsp. red wine vinegar
½ tsp. salt
¼ tsp. pepper
1 tsp. oregano
1 tsp. basil
3 c. pasta spirals, cooked and drained
1 can (20 oz.) chick-peas, drained and rinsed (or 2 c. dried chick-peas, cooked)
1 cup cherry tomatoes, halved (or cubed tomatoes)
4 oz. provolone cheese, cut in thin strips
4 oz. extra-lean ham, cut in thin strips
½ c. pitted ripe olives

1. In a large salad bowl, thoroughly mix the oil, vinegar, salt, pepper, oregano and basil. Add the remaining ingredients and toss to combine.
2. Cover and chill several hours or overnight. Toss; let stand at room temperature for 30 minutes before serving, if possible.

1 serving = 514 calories

SPINACH SALAD WITH CHEESE

4 servings

This salad can be eaten as a refreshing cold main dish meal when cheese is included, or as a side salad if you prefer to omit the cheese. Spinach is very high in vitamin A, beta-carotene, potassium, and iron, and cheese is high in calcium and protein. It makes a great meal when served with whole grain bread and a fruit dessert.

Since spinach doesn't last long in the icebox, I always plan to use it right away or within a day.

2 pkgs. fresh spinach, washed and broken into bite-sized pieces
    (or 1 pkg. spinach for a side salad)
½ lb. fresh mushrooms, sliced
1 can (8 oz.) water chestnuts, sliced
2 chopped hard-boiled eggs
1 small onion, sliced
8 oz. Swiss cheese, cubed

DRESSING

¼ c. red wine vinegar
⅓ c. sugar
¼ c. safflower oil
⅛ tsp. onion powder
½ Tbsp. Worcestershire sauce
2½ Tbsp. catsup

1. Combine vinegar and sugar in a small saucepan and heat until sugar melts. Add all remaining dressing ingredients and mix well.
2. Combine salad ingredients in a large bowl; toss with salad dressing and serve immediately. Garnish with croutons if desired.

1 serving = 356 calories with cheese (not including dressing)
            131 calories without cheese and made with only 1 pkg. spinach
                (not including dressing)
1 Tbsp. dressing = 54 calories (recipe makes 15 Tbsp.)

TAHINI-YOGURT-LEMON SAUCE

1 ¾ cups

This sauce is wonderful as a vegetable dip or sauce for lightly steamed vegetables. Try it when you want to make your vegetables special.

¾ c. sesame tahini
¾ c. plain low-fat yogurt
1 medium clove garlic, crushed or minced
¼ c. lemon juice (2 lemons)
¼ c. scallions, finely minced (optional)
2 Tbsp. parsley flakes
a dash of cayenne
a dash of paprika
a dash of soy sauce
salt to taste

Combine all ingredients in a small bowl and beat well with a wire whisk or wooden spoon. Serve either chilled or at room temperature.

1 Tbsp. = 44 calories

LEMON-GARLIC SAUCE FOR VEGETABLES

12 Tbsp.

This flavorful sauce can be prepared ahead of time and served with either raw or lightly steamed vegetables to turn them into gourmet delights! I like it on broccoli, but you can use it on any vegetable or as a dip. It is also delicious on baked fish.

½ c. mayonnaise
¼ c. lemon juice (2 lemons)
2–3 medium cloves of garlic, crushed or finely chopped
¼ tsp. dry mustard
½ tsp. soy sauce

1. In a small bowl, combine all ingredients with a small wire whisk or
   fork, blending well.
2. If you have ice, chill for at least ½ hour to let flavors blend.
3. Serve over steamed vegetables or fish, or in a small bowl as a dipping sauce for raw or steamed vegetables.

1 Tbsp. = 68 calories with regular mayonnaise
          35 calories with reduced calorie mayonnaise

5

DESSERTS

Since most desserts are composed primarily of fat, sugar, and flour, they are rather deficient nutritionally, with more calories than nutrients. However, you can improve the nutritional status of your desserts by using recipes that include fruits, vegetables, milk, yogurt, or whole grains. I've used whole wheat flour instead of white flour in all of my recipes because personally, I prefer to get a boost of fiber from the whole grain flour. If you prefer lighter and higher cakes, you can use white flour, or a mixture of whole wheat and white flour.

I've included some recipes containing blackstrap molasses because it's the most nutritious sweetener you can use. It has as much iron per tablespoon as 3 ounces of hamburger! However, due to its strong flavor, you can't use it in all recipes. I've tried, and it doesn't work!

Most of my recipes are much lower in fat than traditional recipes of the same type, yet they taste just as good. Any time you decrease fat, you decrease the calories considerably. My Carrot-Orange Cake has 323 calories per serving, whereas I calculate a traditional carrot cake recipe at 815 calories per serving! The calorie difference is mainly due to the difference in the amount of oil used. Beware of recipes that call for 1½ cups of oil, unless you are trying to gain weight!

CALCIUM

Calcium is vital for building and maintaining strong bones, and most people don't get enough of it at home, let alone at sea. The recommended daily allowances of calcium are 800 mg for children and most adults, and 1200 mg for teenagers and pregnant or nursing women. Many experts are now recommending that post-menopausal women also consume 1000 to 1500 mg of calcium daily to prevent osteoporosis, a painful, bone-thinning disease.

If you look at the accompanying chart, you can see what the best sources of calcium are. I recommend keeping a good supply of cheese and nonfat dry milk on board, as well as sardines and salmon, if you like those. Nonfat dry milk can be used to make yogurt (see page 6), included in several of my dessert recipes. It can also be used to make puddings, custard, milk drinks, and cottage cheese (see page 7).

Here's how Rick and I typically get the calcium we need on our sailboat:

Breakfast—1 c. cocoa made with nonfat dry milk	300 mg
Lunch—1 oz. Swiss cheese in a sandwich	275 mg
Dinner—1 c. yogurt for dessert	400 mg
Total =	975 mg

GOOD SEAGOING SOURCES OF CALCIUM

Food	Approximate Milligrams Calcium	Serving Size
Yogurt	400	1 cup
Milkshake	400	10 oz.
Sardines, with bones	375	3 oz.
Milk (whole, low-fat, or skim)	300	1 cup
Cheese		
Swiss	275	1 oz.
cheddar, colby, brick,		
Monterey, Muenster, edam	200	1 oz.
American	175	1 oz.
Soup, made with milk	175	1 cup
Salmon, with bones	165	3 oz.
Collard greens, cooked	150	½ cup
Custard, baked	150	½ cup
Tofu, processed with calcium sulfate	145	4 oz.
Molasses, blackstrap	135	1 Tbsp.
Pudding	130	½ cup
Turnip greens, cooked	125	½ cup
Oysters, raw	110	7–9
Mustard greens, cooked	100	½ cup
Beans, dried, cooked	90	1 cup
Ice cream, ice milk	85	½ cup
Cottage cheese, 2% low-fat	80	½ cup
Kale, cooked	80	½ cup

DIPPING STRAWBERRIES

4 servings

This scrumptious and nutritious dessert provides plenty of vitamin C and calcium. When strawberries are in season, you may find this light dessert to be one of your favorites. Place strawberries in one bowl, yogurt in another and brown sugar in a third and let everyone dig in!

1 qt. (4 c.) fresh, ripe strawberries
1 c. plain, low-fat yogurt
1 tsp. vanilla
3 Tbsp. brown sugar

1. Wash and dry whole strawberries, place in a decorative bowl, and set on the cockpit table.
2. Combine yogurt and vanilla in a small bowl and place next to the strawberries.
3. Put brown sugar in a third small bowl and place next to the strawberries and yogurt. Tell everyone to dip the strawberries in the yogurt, then the brown sugar. Enjoy!

1 serving = 116 calories

STRABERRIES ROMANOFF

6 servings

This is a delightful low-calorie dessert—high in vitamin C, fiber, and calcium. It's also very easy to make. I substitute yogurt for the traditional high-fat whipped cream and sour cream.

1½ *lbs. firm, ripe strawberries, washed, dried, stemmed and quartered lengthwise (reserve 6 whole berries with stems for garnishing)*
¼ *c. Cointreau, Grand Marnier or Triple Sec*
¼ *c. sugar (or to taste)*

TOPPING

1½ *c. plain, low-fat yogurt*
2 *Tbsp. Cointreau, Grand Marnier or Triple Sec*
½ *tsp. vanilla*
3 *Tbsp. chopped pistachio nuts (optional)*

1. At least 4 hours before serving time, combine the berries and liqueur in a large bowl and sprinkle them with sugar. Mix gently with a spoon; cover and place in the icebox. Spoon the syrup over the berries once or twice during cooling time.
2. In a small bowl, combine all topping ingredients except the nuts. Chill until serving time.
3. To serve, place strawberries in dessert dishes and add the topping and nuts. Garnish with reserved whole strawberries.

1 *serving* = 172 *calories with nuts*
149 *calories without nuts*

BLUEBERRY
OR OTHER FRUIT CRISP

6 servings

If you sail "down east" to Maine, you might find yourself picking blueberries. Here's a great recipe to use them in. If you can't find blueberries, you can use apples, pears, peaches or other berries. This recipe can be either baked in the oven or cooked on the stovetop.

3 c. fresh or frozen blueberries or other sliced fruit
2 Tbsp. lemon juice
½ tsp. cinnamon
½ c. packed brown sugar
¾ c. oatmeal
½ c. cornmeal
⅓ c. safflower oil

Oven Method

1. Place blueberries in a lightly oiled or nonstick-sprayed 2-quart casserole dish. Sprinkle with lemon juice and cinnamon and stir.
2. In a small bowl, combine brown sugar, oatmeal, cornmeal and oil. Spread over blueberries or other sliced fruit.
3. Bake at 300° for about 50 minutes or until brown.

Stove Top Method

1. In a small saucepan combine oatmeal, cornmeal and oil. Cook over medium heat for a few minutes. Add brown sugar and cook until grains are lightly browned, stirring frequently.
2. Place blueberries or sliced fruit in the bottom of a large, lightly oiled or nonstick-sprayed skillet. Sprinkle with lemon juice and cinnamon, stir and heat through.
3. Spread the oatmeal mixture over the fruit, cover and heat for a few minutes, then serve.

1 serving = 284 calories

MERINGUE BOWLS WITH FRESH FRUIT

6 servings

This is by far the most beautiful and delightful dessert I have ever tasted, although it does take some advanced planning. I usually make the meringue bowls at home ahead of time, pack them between paper towels in a square Tupperware container, and transport them to the boat. They're very delicate, so you have to pack them well. If you don't have time to bother with the meringues, you can simply omit them and still use this recipe to make a lovely fruit cup.

Fresh summer fruit makes this dessert healthy. As a special treat Rick and I sometimes allow ourselves the indulgence of whipped cream topping, but the recipe is also delicious (and much healthier) with Honey-Vanilla Yogurt (recipe follows).

4 egg whites, at room temperature
1 tsp. vinegar
¼ tsp. salt
1 c. sugar
1 tsp. vanilla
Whipped cream (optional) or Honey-Vanilla Yogurt (optional)
Fresh or canned fruit of your choice, drained and cut up; I use 1 cantaloupe,
    1 qt. strawberries and/or blueberries, 1 banana, 1 peach, ½ lb. grapes,
    and 1 kiwi fruit
1 Tbsp. sugar
2 Tbsp. liqueur such as Grand Marnier (optional)

MERINGUE BOWLS

1. Combine egg whites, vinegar, and salt in a large bowl. Beat with an egg beater until foamy-white and double in volume. Gradually add sugar, 1 Tbsp. at a time, beating until the meringue stands in stiff peaks. (As the meringue gets stiffer, I switch over to a wire whisk, as it gets difficult using the eggbeater. At home, you can use a mixer to do the whole job.)
2. On a lightly greased (or nonstick-sprayed) and floured cookie sheet, spoon meringue into 6 equal circles and press with a spoon to form bowls (to hold fruit later).
3. Bake meringues at 250° for 1 hour. Turn off the oven and allow the meringues to cool there. When cool, loosen the meringues from the cookie sheet with a long spatula. (At this point, meringues are ready to be eaten or may be stored in an airtight container for several days.)

FRUIT CUP

1. Combine fruit (except banana and kiwi) in a large bowl. Add sugar and liqueur, if desired, and stir gently. Serve immediately, or store in the icebox until serving time. Just before serving, add the banana slices.
2. Place meringue bowls on serving plates, fill with fruit and place kiwi slices on top. Top with whipped cream or Honey-Vanilla Yogurt, if desired.

1 serving = 226 calories (not including whipped cream or yogurt)

HONEY-VANILLA YOGURT

1 cup

This easy topping is a great way to dress up most fresh or canned fruit.

1 c. plain low-fat yogurt
1 Tbsp. honey
1 tsp. vanilla

Combine all ingredients and serve on top of fruit.

1 Tbsp. = 11 calories

PEACHES
WITH HONEY-LIME YOGURT

6 servings

This is a very refreshing and low-calorie dessert—great after a heavy meal! The peaches provide generous amounts of vitamin A and beta-carotene and the yogurt adds calcium.

6 fresh ripe peaches (or 12 canned halves)
2 Tbsp. honey
2 Tbsp. lime juice
1 tsp. freshly grated lime peel
¾ c. plain low-fat yogurt
a dash of mace or cardamom

1. Cut peaches into halves and place 2 halves into each serving dish.
2. Combine honey, lime juice, lime peel, yogurt, and mace in a small bowl and spoon over peaches, then serve.

1 serving = 102 calories

FRUIT-GRANOLA-YOGURT SUNDAE

1 serving

If you have some fruit, granola, and yogurt available, you can use your imagination to make a wonderfully tasty and nutritious dessert.

any fresh or canned fruit
granola (p. 27)
plain low-fat yogurt
honey, sugar or brown sugar
any flavoring extracts (vanilla, almond, rum, cherry, etc.)
any spices (cinnamon, nutmeg, cloves, allspice, etc.)

1. Combine yogurt with sweetener, flavoring extracts, and spices.
2. Place fruit in the bottom of a serving bowl, then top with yogurt and granola.

1 serving = 219 calories using ½ c. fruit, ½ c. yogurt, 1 tsp. honey or sugar, and ¼ c. granola

APPLE-YOGURT SUNDAE

2 servings

This healthy dessert can be prepared in just a few minutes and tastes delicious. It also makes a great snack.

½ c. plain low-fat yogurt
1½ tsp. honey
2 small, unpeeled apples
2 Tbsp. orange juice
1 Tbsp. raisins
⅛ tsp. cinnamon
a dash of nutmeg

1. In a small bowl, combine the yogurt and honey.
2. Slice apples into small pieces and place in a small bowl. Cover with orange juice. Add raisins and cinnamon and mix well.
3. Divide the fruit into two bowls and pour yogurt on top of the fruit. Sprinkle a dash of cinnamon and nutmeg over each portion and serve.

1 serving = 136 calories

BAKED CUSTARD

5 servings

Custards and puddings provide a great way to get more calcium into your diet. This recipe and the several following are all delicious and easy to make.

1⅓ c. nonfat dry milk powder (or one 1-quart envelope)
2 c. water
2 eggs, beaten with a fork
3 Tbsp. honey or ¼ c. sugar
1 tsp. vanilla
⅛ tsp. nutmeg
a dash of salt
a dash of cinnamon

1. In a large bowl, combine the nonfat dry milk powder with water. (The milk dissolves best with part hot water.) Beat the eggs into the milk with a wire whisk; add the honey or sugar, vanilla, nutmeg and salt.
2. Pour the mixture into 5 lightly oiled or nonstick-sprayed custard cups, or one baking dish. Sprinkle with a dash of cinnamon. Place the cups or dish in a pan of water filled to halfway up the sides of the cups.
3. Bake at 325° for about 50 minutes, or until a knife inserted into the center comes out clean.

   (For flavor variety, omit the vanilla and add 2 tsp. rum or brandy, or a few drops of almond or peppermint extract.)

1 serving = 136 calories

STIRRED CUSTARD

5 servings

3 eggs, slightly beaten
⅓ c. sugar
a dash of salt
2½ c. skim milk
1 tsp. vanilla

1. Blend eggs, sugar, and salt in top of a double boiler, if you have one, or a saucepan. (If you use a saucepan, make sure that it does not burn on the bottom.) Gradually stir in the milk. Cook over medium heat, stirring constantly, for about 20 minutes, or until the mixture just coats a metal spoon. (Water in double boiler should not boil.)
2. Remove top of double boiler from the heat and stir in the vanilla. Serve warm or cooled over fruit such as sliced bananas, orange sections, strawberries, etc.

1 serving = 140 calories (not including fruit)

VANILLA PUDDING

5 servings

⅓ c. sugar
¼ c. cornstarch
⅛ tsp. salt
2¾ c. skim milk
1 Tbsp. liquid corn oil margarine (optional)
1 tsp. vanilla

1. In a large saucepan, combine sugar, cornstarch, and salt. Gradually stir in the milk. Bring to a boil over medium heat, stirring constantly, and boil for 1 minute. Remove from heat.
2. Stir in margarine and vanilla. Chill if you have ice, or serve warm.

1 serving = 143 calories

CHOCOLATE PUDDING

5 servings

Follow the above recipe, but add 3 Tbsp. unsweetened cocoa powder to the sugar-cornstarch-salt mixture before adding milk.

1 serving = 150 *calories*

BUTTERSCOTCH PUDDING

5 servings

Follow the recipe for Vanilla Pudding, but substitute firmly-packed brown sugar for the white sugar and increase margarine to 2 Tbsp.

1 serving = 171 *calories*

APPLE CRISP

4 servings

This recipe provides generous amounts of soluble fiber from the apples and oat bran or oatmeal. Serve warm or chilled with a glass of cold milk.

APPLE LAYER

- 4 c. apple slices
- ¼ c. water
- 4 tsp. firmly packed brown sugar
- 2 tsp. lemon juice
- ¾ tsp. cinnamon

TOPPING

½ c. oat bran or oatmeal
2 Tbsp. chopped walnuts
1 Tbsp. firmly packed brown sugar
1 Tbsp. safflower oil

1. Combine all ingredients in the apple layer and toss lightly to coat apples. Layer on bottom of an 8-inch square baking dish that has been lightly oiled or nonstick-sprayed.
2. Combine all topping ingredients in a small bowl and sprinkle over apples. Bake at 375° for about 30 minutes or until the apples are tender and topping is lightly browned.

1 serving = 178 calories

SPEEDY SPECIAL BANANAS

2 servings

This recipe is great for when you want something sweet yet healthy, and you want it NOW!

2 medium ripe bananas, halved lengthwise
2 Tbsp. lime juice
2 Tbsp. brown sugar
1 Tbsp. sesame seeds
Thin lime slices (optional)

Arrange banana slices on 2 serving plates, cut side up. Sprinkle with lime juice, then brown sugar and sesame seeds. Garnish with lime slices. Serve with a fork.

1 serving = 176 calories

PINEAPPLE FLAMBÉ

6 servings

This lovely dessert is a very easy to prepare and is also low in calories.

1 *ripe pineapple, approximately 3 lbs. (It's ripe if you can detect pineapple aroma when you sniff the bottom.)*
2 *Tbsp. brown sugar*
5 *Tbsp. rum, divided*

1. Cut off the pineapple crown about 2 inches from the top; set aside. With a long, sharp knife, cut around sides of pulp to within ½ inch of the shell and bottom. Twist to remove pulp; cut out and discard the center core, then cut the pulp into cubes. Place shell and crown in the icebox, if you have one.
2. In a medium-sized bowl, combine brown sugar, 3 Tbsp. rum, and pineapple cubes. Let stand at room temperature for at least 1 hour, stirring occasionally.
3. Before serving, spoon pineapple cubes into the pineapple shell, top with the crown, and place on a serving dish. Pour the remaining 2 Tbsp. rum into a ladle, warm the ladle with a candle, and ignite the rum. Remove the pineapple crown and carefully pour the flaming rum over the pineapple cubes in the shell, then spoon into serving dishes.

1 *serving* = 78 *calories*

PUMPKIN PIE

8 servings

This delicious pie is low in saturated fat and cholesterol and very high in vitamin A, beta-carotene and calcium. If you don't feel like making a crust and want to save a lot of calories, simply pour the pumpkin mixture into an oiled or nonstick-sprayed pie pan and bake.

⅔ c. packed brown sugar
¾ tsp. cinnamon
¼ tsp. ginger
⅛ tsp. cloves
1½ c. pumpkin (1 lb. can)
1 can (13 oz.) evaporated skim milk
3 egg whites, beaten with a wire whisk until foamy
1 Whole Wheat Pie Crust (p. 56)

1. In a large bowl, combine brown sugar, spices, and pumpkin. Add milk and egg whites and mix thoroughly. Pour mixture into a pastry-lined pan.
2. Bake at 400° for 45 to 50 minutes or until a knife inserted into center of pie comes out clean.

1 serving = 248 calories with crust
            135 calories without crust

OATMEAL-WALNUT CAKE

12 servings

This wonderful cake provides fiber and B vitamins from the oatmeal and whole wheat flour. Serve with a glass of cold milk.

1½ c. boiling water
1 c. raw oatmeal
1½ c. whole wheat flour
1 tsp. baking soda
1 tsp. cinnamon
1 tsp. nutmeg
½ c. liquid corn oil margarine
1 c. sugar
1 c. brown sugar, firmly packed
2 eggs
1 tsp. vanilla

TOPPING

3 Tbsp. liquid corn oil margarine
¾ c. brown sugar, firmly packed
¾ c. walnuts, coarsely chopped
1 egg
3 Tbsp. skim milk

1. In a small bowl, pour boiling water over oatmeal and stir with a fork to mix well. Let stand while the rest of the cake is being prepared.
2. In a small bowl, mix together flour, soda, cinnamon, and nutmeg.
3. In a large bowl, cream margarine, sugar, and brown sugar together.
4. Beat in 2 eggs, one at a time, until mixture is light and fluffy. Beat in vanilla.
5. Add oatmeal mixture and beat well.
6. Gradually beat in flour mixture until well combined.
7. Turn batter into a lightly oiled or nonstick-sprayed and floured 9-inch by 9-inch by 2-inch baking pan.
8. Bake at 350° for 50 minutes, or until top springs back when gently pressed with fingertip.
9. Meanwhile, combine all topping ingredients in a small bowl. Spread over hot cake.
10. Return cake to oven and bake 10 minutes longer, or until topping is golden.

1 serving = 396 calories

BANANA CAKE

9 servings

This cake is really easy to make because you mix up the cake ingredients in the baking pan and there are no mixing bowls to wash! It also provides a great way to use up any extra bananas you may have around. The bananas provide potassium and the whole wheat flour supplies fiber and B vitamins.

1 ¼ c. whole wheat flour
⅔ c. sugar
¼ c. cornstarch
1 tsp. baking soda
½ tsp. salt
1 c. mashed ripe bananas (about 2 medium bananas)
⅓ c. safflower oil
1 egg, slightly beaten with a fork
1 Tbsp. vinegar
1 tsp. vanilla

FROSTING

¼ c. liquid corn oil margarine
1 c. confectioners' sugar
1 tsp. lemon juice
1 small banana, sliced and placed in a small bowl with 1 Tbsp. lemon juice and
    1 tsp. sugar (to prevent darkening)

1. In an 8-inch or 9-inch square pan, thoroughly mix flour, sugar, cornstarch, baking soda, and salt. Add remaining ingredients except frosting and blend well.
2. Bake at 350° for 30 to 35 minutes or until a toothpick inserted comes out clean. Cool in the pan on a rack.
3. To make the frosting, cream margarine, confectioners' sugar and lemon juice together in a small bowl. In another bowl, combine sliced bananas with the lemon juice and sugar.
4. After the cake has cooled, spread with frosting and top with banana slices.

1 serving = 337 calories

CARROT-ORANGE CAKE

12 servings

This delightful, moist cake is full of good things — vitamin A and beta-carotene in the carrots, fiber in the whole wheat flour and the carrots, and vitamin C in the orange juice.

3 c. whole wheat flour
2 tsp. baking powder
1 tsp. baking soda
½ tsp. salt
1 tsp. cinnamon
½ tsp. nutmeg
¾ c. brown sugar, firmly packed
¼ c. safflower oil
1 ¼ c. orange juice
3 eggs, beaten with a fork
1 tsp. vanilla
2 c. (½ lb.) carrots, finely shredded
½ c. chopped walnuts
¼ c. raisins

TOPPING

¼ c. orange juice
¼ c. brown sugar, firmly packed
2 Tbsp. confectioners' sugar

1. In a large bowl, combine the first six ingredients and mix well.
2. Add the remaining ingredients except the topping, mixing well after each addition.
3. Pour the batter into a 9-inch square pan which has been lightly oiled or nonstick-sprayed. Bake at 350° for about 50 minutes or until a toothpick inserted comes out clean.
4. Meanwhile, combine topping ingredients. After the cake has baked for 15 minutes, pour the topping evenly over it. Return cake to the oven for 35 more minutes or until done.

1 serving = 323 calories

GINGERBREAD

9 servings

Because of its high iron content, molasses is the most nutritious sweetener you can use. In this recipe, the cake is sweetened entirely with blackstrap molasses, resulting in an iron content per serving equal to that found in a 3-ounce portion of meat. I have also reduced the oil content, to decrease the fat and calories — yet the cake is very moist and delicious. It also provides fiber from the whole wheat flour and can be made in a flash.

¼ c. safflower oil
1 c. blackstrap molasses
1 tsp. baking soda
¼ tsp. salt
1 tsp. ginger
1 tsp. cinnamon
1 egg, unbeaten
1½ c. whole wheat flour
1 c. water
1 Tbsp. confectioners' sugar

1. Using a measuring cup, pour the oil into a large bowl, coating the measuring cup as you do so; then measure the molasses in the same cup so that it will slide right out. Add baking soda, salt, ginger, cinnamon and egg; mix well. Add the flour and water and mix thoroughly.
2. Spread batter into an oiled or nonstick-sprayed 9-inch square baking pan and bake at 350° for 30 to 35 minutes or until a toothpick inserted comes out clean. Sprinkle confectioners' sugar on the top and serve warm or cold.

1 serving = 227 calories

CHOCOLATE CAKE
WITH CHOCOLATE SAUCE

9 servings

This unusual recipe features a cake that makes its own sauce. It reminds you of eating brownies drenched in chocolate syrup. However, the syrup and cake are made from cocoa powder instead of chocolate so that the dessert is low in saturated fat and total fat.

1 c. whole wheat flour
¾ c. sugar
2 tsp. baking powder
2 Tbsp. safflower oil
3 Tbsp. cocoa powder
½ c. skim milk
½ tsp. vanilla
½ c. packed brown sugar
½ c. sugar
¼ c. cocoa powder
1½ c. cold water or coffee

1. In a large bowl, combine flour, sugar, and baking powder. Combine oil and cocoa and add to dry ingredients. Beat in milk and vanilla.
2. Pour batter into a lightly oiled or nonstick-sprayed 9-inch square baking pan. Sprinkle the remaining dry ingredients over the top of the batter one at a time, but do not mix. Pour coffee or water over the top.
3. Bake at 350° for 40 minutes. To serve, invert each piece on a serving plate.

1 *serving* = 246 *calories*

SKILLET POPPY SEED CAKE

8 servings

I like to prepare this easy, tasty, low-fat cake right before I plan to serve dinner. It bakes on the stovetop while we're eating our meal and tastes wonderful when served warm, right from the pan.

½ c. poppy seeds (2¼ oz. box)
½ c. skim milk
1 c. whole wheat flour
2 tsp. baking powder
½ c. packed brown sugar
2 eggs, beaten with a fork
1 tsp. vanilla
1 Tbsp. safflower oil
2 Tbsp. confectioners' sugar (optional)

1. Combine poppy seeds and milk in a cup and let sit while batter is being prepared.
2. In a large bowl, combine flour, baking powder and brown sugar. Stir in poppy seed mixture and add eggs, vanilla and oil. Mix thoroughly.
3. Pour batter into an oiled or nonstick-sprayed frying pan. Bake on a trivet over very low heat with cover ajar ½ inch for 50 minutes or until top is done and a toothpick inserted comes out clean.
4. If desired, sprinkle with confectioners' sugar. Serve either warm or cold.

1 serving = 199 calories

PUMPKIN-WALNUT COOKIES

5 dozen

These delightful soft cookies are high in fiber, vitamin A and beta-carotene. They are easy to make, too!

½ c. liquid corn oil margarine (1 stick)
1½ c. brown sugar, firmly packed
2 eggs
1 can (15 oz.) pumpkin or squash (or 1½ c. cooked)
1 tsp. vanilla
1 tsp. lemon juice
3 c. whole wheat flour
3 tsp. baking powder
½ tsp. salt
1 tsp. cinnamon
¼ tsp. ginger
⅛ tsp. cloves
1 c. walnuts, coarsely chopped

1. In a large bowl, cream the margarine and brown sugar together until fluffy. Beat in eggs, one at a time. Stir in pumpkin, vanilla, and lemon juice.
2. In a small bowl, combine flour with baking powder, salt and spices. Add to pumpkin mixture. Stir in walnuts.
3. Drop batter by rounded teaspoonfuls 2 inches apart onto a lightly oiled or nonstick-sprayed cookie sheet. Bake at 375° for 12 to 14 minutes.

1 cookie = 76 calories

OATMEAL-BANANA-RAISIN COOKIES

4 dozen

These wonderful soft cookies are high in fiber, potassium, and B vitamins and provide a good way to use up ripe bananas.

½ c. liquid corn oil margarine
1 c. sugar
1 egg
2 large mashed ripe bananas (about 1⅓ c.)
½ tsp. soda
½ tsp. cinnamon
¼ tsp. salt
¼ tsp. nutmeg
1½ c. whole wheat flour
1½ c. oatmeal
½ c. raisins
½ c. walnuts, chopped (optional)

1. In a large bowl, cream the margarine and sugar. Beat in egg, then add remaining ingredients until well mixed.
2. Drop by rounded teaspoonfuls, 2 inches apart, onto a lightly oiled or nonstick-sprayed cookie sheet.
3. Bake at 400° for 10 to 12 minutes or until golden brown.

1 cookie = 77 calories

ZUCCHINI BREAD

2 loaves

This recipe for zucchini bread is chock-full of zucchini and low in fat.

3 *eggs*
¼ *c. oil*
1 *c. sugar*
3 *c. grated zucchini (about 1 lb.)*
1 *Tbsp. vanilla*
1 *tsp. salt*
1 *tsp. baking soda*
1 *tsp. cinnamon*
¼ *tsp. baking powder*
¼ *c. water*
3 *c. whole wheat flour*

1. In a large bowl, combine eggs and oil and beat until foamy. Add sugar, zucchini, and vanilla and mix well. Add remaining ingredients one at a time, stirring after each addition.
2. Pour mixture into 2 oiled or nonstick-sprayed bread pans and bake at 350° for 50 to 60 minutes or until done.

¹⁄₁₂ of one loaf = 129 calories

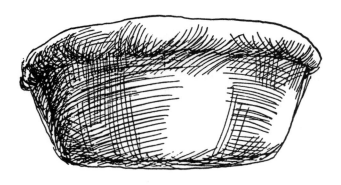

HIBACHI DESSERT KABOBS

This is an easy, healthy, and fun dessert to complete your hibachi meal.

1 c. plain low-fat yogurt
1 Tbsp. honey
¼ tsp. ground ginger
1½ tsp. cinnamon
1 medium-sized firm-ripe cantaloupe
½ large firm-ripe honeydew melon
2 large almost-ripe bananas
leftover angel cake or other noncrumbly dessert cake, cut into 1-inch cubes
  (optional)
4 Tbsp. liquid corn oil margarine
2 Tbsp. brown sugar

1. Combine yogurt, honey, ginger and ½ tsp. of the cinnamon. Set aside.
2. Cut melons and bananas into 1-inch cubes. Thread melon, banana pieces and cake (if you have it) onto 6 skewers.
3. In a small skillet, melt margarine and stir in brown sugar. Cook, stirring constantly, until the sugar melts. Stir in the remaining 1 tsp. cinnamon. Brush mixture on skewers.
4. Grill over hot coals for about 5 minutes or until golden, turning once and brushing with margarine. Serve warm with yogurt sauce.

1 *serving* = 243 *calorie*

6

SNACKS

Snacks can be real hazards to navigation, nutritionally speaking. When people think of snacks, what usually come to mind are things such as potato chips, cookies, and candy bars, and since these foods are also convenient to store and keep on a boat, they wind up being the featured items at most cockpit snack breaks. But these junk foods contribute little to your diet except calories and are often high in cholesterol, saturated fat, and salt as well. In this chapter you'll find many ideas for snacks that are tasty and satisfying, yet healthful. Several of these recipes are particularly appropriate when there are children aboard, and some are so simple that children can make them themselves. For adults, you'll find recipes for delicious appetizers and dips to try either underway or while at anchor waiting for the evening meal to cook. Once you've caught the spirit of nutritious snacking, let your imagination be your guide. You'll soon be supplementing these ideas with tasty recipes of your own.

HEALTHY SNACK FOODS TO BRING ABOARD

For purchased snack foods, I suggest the following:

Low-fat yogurt
Cheese with crackers or skewered with fruit
Fresh fruits
Dried fruits — plain or mixed with nuts and seeds
Raw vegetables with dips (recipes follow)
Graham crackers
Whole grain crackers
Popcorn (pop it yourself in safflower oil)
Nuts and seeds

Although dried fruits are much more nutritious than candy, they stick tenaciously to the teeth. You should brush after a dried fruit snack.

If you have an unquenchable urge for a salty snack, pretzels are a better choice than potato chips because they contain less fat. Better yet, why not try my recipe for Potato Crisps (below) or for Herbed Crunch (page 151). If you're in the mood for sweet snacks, this chapter includes recipes for granola bars, nutty popcorn balls, and healthful candy substitutes, as well as suggestions on how to turn nonfat dry milk into a tasty snack beverage. You'll find many other ideas for sweet snacks in the dessert chapter. In particular, you might want to try some of the tasty cookie recipes, whip up a delicious Apple-Yogurt Sundae (page 129) or even bake Zucchini Bread (page 144).

As for dips, in addition to the recipes listed here, don't forget Tahini-Yogurt-Lemon Sauce (page 118) and Lemon-Garlic Sauce (page 119). Although I usually use these as vegetable sauces, they both make terrific dips.

POTATO CRISPS

4 servings

These are just like thick potato chips with no fat.

4 baking potatoes
paprika
onion and/or garlic powder
salt (optional)

1. Scrub potatoes and bake at 400° for 40 to 60 minutes or until done. Place in the icebox for a few hours until very cold.
2. Cut each potato into round slices, ¼-inch thick. Place the slices on a nonstick-sprayed cookie sheet and sprinkle with paprika, onion and/or garlic powder. Bake at 400° for about 20 minutes on each side or until crisp. Salting is optional.

1 serving = *100 calories (approximately)*

NO-FAT FRENCH FRIES

4 servings

These french fries are easier to make than traditional greasy fries and are much healthier too.

4 baking potatoes

Scrub potatoes and slice into french fries. Place on a nonstick sprayed cookie sheet and bake at 400° for about 20 minutes or until tender. Then place under the broiler for about 4 minutes on each side to brown.

1 serving = 100 calories (approximately)

PARMESAN POPCORN

4 servings

We like to keep popcorn aboard in case we get the urge for a crunchy snack. Popcorn is high in fiber and relatively low in calories. The cheese replaces traditional salt and butter.

½ c. popping corn
2 Tbsp. safflower oil
¼ c. freshly grated parmesan or romano cheese

1. Put popping corn and oil in a large saucepan and shake to coat the corn with oil. Cover and cook over high heat, shaking while the corn pops.
2. Put popcorn in a large bowl and sprinkle with the cheese.

1 serving = 169 calories

NUTTY POPCORN BALLS

10 balls

This is a fun snack for kids to make from ingredients you might have on hand on your boat.

1 c. blackstrap molasses
½ c. sugar
1 Tbsp. vinegar
⅛ tsp. salt
1 Tbsp. liquid corn oil margarine
popcorn from above recipe (minus the cheese)
½ c. peanuts

1. In a medium saucepan, combine molasses, sugar, vinegar, and salt. Boil until a small amount of the mixture turns brittle when dropped in cold water (about 270° if you happen to have a cooking thermometer aboard).
2. Add margarine and pour mixture over popcorn and peanuts in a large bowl. Stir gently until coated. When cool enough to handle, press into balls. Wrap cooled balls in plastic wrap to store.

1 ball = 210 calories

HERBED CRUNCH

4½ cups

This tasty snack food contains virtually no salt.

- ¼ *c. margarine*
- 1½ *tsp. oregano*
- 1½ *tsp. dried basil*
- ½ *tsp. garlic powder*
- ½ *tsp. onion powder*
- 3 *c. bite-sized shredded wheat*
- 1 *c. unsalted peanuts*

1. Melt margarine in a skillet over moderate heat until melted.
2. Stir in seasonings. Add peanuts and shredded wheat and toss until evenly coated with the margarine mixture.

¼ cup = 97 calories

ENGLISH MUFFIN PIZZAS

4 servings

These quick pizzas are great for meals or snacks. If desired, sautéed vegetables such as mushrooms, green peppers, and onions can be added on top of the sauce.

- 2 *whole wheat English muffins or 2 (2 oz.) pocket breads*
- ½ *c. pizza sauce, tomato sauce, or tomato paste*
- 4 *oz. part-skim mozzarella cheese*

1. Split English muffins or pocket breads in half and place on a cookie sheet. Spread each half with pizza sauce and top with 1 oz. cheese.
2. Bake at 350° for about 8 minutes or until cheese bubbles.

1 serving = 181 calories

NACHOS

6 servings

This easy and delightful recipe works equally well as an appetizer, snack, or part of a meal. You can vary the recipe by adding refried beans under the taco sauce and cheese. Kids love them!

1 *pkg. (8 oz.) round tortilla chips*
4 *oz. taco sauce (as mild or hot as you like it)*
8 *oz. shredded Monterey Jack cheese*

1. Spread tortilla chips out on cookie sheets or foil pan. Cover each tortilla chip with a little taco sauce and top with cheese. Broil until cheese melts, about 2 to 3 minutes. Serve immediately.

1 *generous serving* = 295 *calories (not including refried beans)*

CHILI DIP

2½ cups

1 *can (16 oz.) tomatoes*
1 *large onion, chopped*
2 *cans (4 oz. each) chopped green chili peppers, drained*
½ *tsp. salt*
1 *tsp. chili powder*
1 *c. plain low-fat yogurt*

1. In a large saucepan, break up tomatoes and cook over medium heat with onion, chili peppers, salt, and chili powder until onion is soft.
2. Turn off heat and stir in yogurt. Serve immediately with tortilla chips.

1 *Tbsp.* = 7 *calories*

GUACAMOLE

3 cups

This guacamole tastes rich in sour cream, but it contains no sour cream at all, just plain yogurt instead. The yogurt stretches the guacamole so that it has less fat and fewer calories—only 43 per ¼ cup as opposed to the 128 per ¼ cup for traditional guacamole. Besides being a great dip, guacamole also goes well with tacos and other Mexican dishes (see pages 61–62).

1 large ripe avocado
1 large chopped tomato
1 large chopped green pepper
1 tsp. chili powder
⅛ tsp. onion powder
1 Tbsp. lime juice
1 c. plain low-fat yogurt
salt to taste

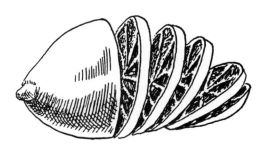

1. In a medium-sized bowl, mash the peeled avocado with a fork. Blend in remaining ingredients except yogurt. Spread part of the yogurt on top to prevent darkening.
2. Just before serving, stir in the remaining yogurt.

¼ c. = 43 calories

INSTANT DIP

1 cup

1 c. low-fat cottage cheese
¼ pkg. onion soup mix or 1 oz. crumbled blue cheese

Combine cottage cheese and onion soup mix or blue cheese and mix well with a fork. Serve with raw vegetables or whole grain crackers.

1 Tbsp. = 12 calories with onion soup
14 calories with blue cheese

BEAU MONDE DIP

2 cups

1 c. mayonnaise
1 c. plain low-fat yogurt
2 Tbsp. dill weed
4 Tbsp. parsley flakes
2 tsp. Beau Monde seasoning (found in some grocery stores and gourmet specialty stores)

Combine all ingredients and chill. Serve with raw vegetables or bread. (For a really special presentation, hollow out the center of a loaf of pumpernickel bread, fill the hollow with dip, and use the remaining bread cubes as dippers.)

1 Tbsp. = 52 calories with regular mayonnaise
        27 calories with reduced-calorie mayonnaise

CHEESE-CARROT SPREAD

1 cup

½ c. grated carrots
½ c. grated cheddar cheese (2 oz.)
2 Tbsp. mayonnaise
2 tsp. lemon juice

Combine all ingredients in a small bowl and mix well. Serve as a spread for whole grain crackers or stuffed celery.

1 Tbsp. = 27 calories

TASTY VEGETABLE DIP

1 ⅓ cups

This easy dip is low in sodium but you won't miss it one bit!

⅔ c. mayonnaise
⅔ c. plain low-fat yogurt
1 Tbsp. dried parsley flakes
1 tsp. dill weed
⅛ tsp. each garlic powder, onion powder, and celery seed

Combine all ingredients and mix well. Cover and chill for several hours to blend flavors, if you have ice. Serve with raw vegetables.

1 Tbsp. = 52 calories with regular mayonnaise
27 calories with reduced-calorie mayonnaise

MOLASSES CAKES

8 servings

These delicious cakes can be made on the stovetop for snacks, and leftovers can be eaten for breakfast. They are great plain or with peanut butter and/or jelly. The molasses provides iron and the whole wheat flour provides fiber.

1½ c. whole wheat flour
¼ tsp. salt
½ tsp. baking soda
½ tsp. cream of tartar
½ tsp. cinnamon
½ tsp. ginger
¼ c. liquid corn oil margarine (½ stick)
¼ c. skim milk
¼ tsp. vinegar or lemon juice
¼ c. blackstrap molasses

1. In a medium-sized bowl, combine flour, salt, baking soda, cream of tartar, cinnamon, and ginger. Mix well. Cut in the margarine with a pastry cutter or fork until mixture forms crumbs.
2. Pour the milk and vinegar or lemon juice into a 1-cup measure and add the molasses. Stir well. Add to the flour mixture to make a stiff dough.
3. Pat or roll the dough into a ½-inch thick circle onto a piece of waxed paper or foil. Cut into 8 triangles.
4. Oil a skillet (or use a nonstick spray) and heat over low to medium heat. Sprinkle surface lightly with flour. Bake molasses cakes for 4 minutes on each side. Serve warm or cold.

1 *serving* = 166 *calories*

PEANUT BUTTER–
GRANOLA BARS

32 bars

These bars fit the bill when you or your children want something sweet and satisfying, yet good for you. Since they get soft at room temperature, it's best to store them in the icebox.

1 c. granola (see page 27)
1 c. nonfat dry milk powder
½ c. packed brown sugar
¼ tsp. salt (optional)
½ c. raisins
½ c. sunflower seeds
½ c. sesame seeds
2½ c. natural peanut butter

1. Combine all ingredients in a large bowl, adding peanut butter last and mixing it in with your hands.
2. Press mixture into a large rectangular cake pan (or 2 smaller pans) and chill in the icebox.
3. When firm, cut into 32 bars or squares and wrap each in plastic wrap. Store in a covered container in the icebox.

1 *bar* = 182 *calories*

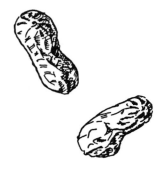

COCOA-WALNUT GRANOLA BARS

2 dozen

These easy, cocoa-flavored granola bars are a good low-saturated-fat alternative to bars with chocolate chips added.

¼ c. liquid corn oil margarine (½ stick)
¾ c. packed brown sugar
⅓ c. light corn syrup
1 egg
1 tsp. vanilla
½ c. dry cocoa powder
3 c. oatmeal
½ c. chopped walnuts

1. In a large bowl, beat together margarine, brown sugar, and corn syrup until light and fluffy. Blend in egg, vanilla, and cocoa powder, then oatmeal and walnuts. Mix well.
2. Press mixture firmly into an oiled or nonstick-sprayed 9-inch square baking pan.
3. Bake at 350° for 25 to 30 minutes. Cool on a wire rack. If possible, chill in the icebox for at least 1 hour before cutting. Cut into 24 bars.

1 bar = 117 calories

QUICK COCOA-OATMEAL CHEWIES

2 dozen

These are great when you're in the mood for candy. The recipe is so easy and quick that even children can make it without too much trouble. Although these chewies taste like rich chocolate, they contain no saturated fat at all.

1 c. sugar
3 Tbsp. dry cocoa powder
½ c. nonfat dry milk powder
2 Tbsp. liquid corn oil margarine
¼ c. water
¼ c. natural peanut butter
1 tsp. vanilla
1½ c. oatmeal

1. In a large saucepan, bring sugar, cocoa, nonfat dry milk, margarine, and water to a boil. Boil and stir 2 minutes. Add peanut butter and stir until melted. Add vanilla and oatmeal and mix thoroughly.
2. Drop by rounded teaspoonfuls onto waxed paper or foil. (Use a knife to push the mixture off the spoon so that you don't burn yourself.) Cool and eat.

1 chewie = 82 calories

PEANUT BUTTER CANDIES

2 dozen

Although this recipe is a little messy to make, it sure beats regular candy nutritionally, providing protein, B vitamins, and calcium.

⅓ c. honey
½ c. natural peanut butter
½ c. nonfat dry milk powder

1. Mix honey and peanut butter together in a medium-sized bowl. Stir in nonfat dry milk, a little at a time, until thoroughly blended.
2. Spread mixture into a long roll on a sheet of waxed paper. Wrap paper into a long roll and seal sides and ends. Chill on ice until firm.
3. When roll is firm, slice into 24 pieces. Wrap each piece in plastic wrap and store in a covered container in the icebox.

1 piece = 52 calories

NONFAT DRY MILK DRINKS

These are good ways to get calcium if you live aboard and don't have an icebox.

In a jar, shake together ⅓ c. nonfat dry milk powder with slightly less than 1 c. water. Flavor in any of the following ways:

- Add about ½ tsp. of one or more of the following extracts: vanilla, almond, maple, chocolate, coffee, or strawberry. Add a little sugar, honey, or molasses to sweeten, if desired.

- *Chocolate milk* — Add dark cocoa powder to milk and sweeten to taste.

- *Hot cocoa* — Heat the above recipe, or use the recipe for homemade cocoa mix (below).

- *Hot mocha* — Add 1 tsp. instant coffee to the cocoa.

- *Cinnamon cocoa* — Add a couple of shakes of cinnamon (or a cinnamon stick) to the cocoa recipe.

- *Ambrosia shake* — Mash 1 ripe banana until smooth and creamy. Add ¼ c. orange juice, ½ tsp. vanilla, and 1 c. reconstituted nonfat dry milk. Mix well and enjoy!

- *Banana shake* — Omit orange juice from the above recipe.

- *Orange milk* — Mix together 1 c. reconstituted nonfat dry milk, ½ c. orange juice, and 1 tsp. vanilla.

HOMEMADE COCOA MIX

8 servings

If you find yourself out of cocoa mix, you can easily make your own!

⅓ c. sugar
⅓ c. dry cocoa powder
¼ tsp. salt
2 envelopes nonfat dry milk powder (or 2⅔ c.)

Combine all ingredients and store in an airtight container. When in the mood for hot cocoa, measure a heaping ¼ c. into a mug and fill with boiling water.

1 serving = 119 calories

7

Menu Planning and Provisioning

A commitment to eating good food afloat is also a commitment to a bit of advance planning. If you're like most cruising sailors, the attractiveness of convenience foods lies in the fact that you can simply pile an assortment of cans into the food locker and know that *something* will be there to eat. But if you want meals that are both good tasting and nutritionally complete, you can't just start with assorted items; you have to start with menu plans. It's inefficient and wasteful of precious cabin space to stock up on perishable fruits and vegetables with no idea of how—or if—you're going to use them. Even worse is to be planning a specific dish for dinner and discover that an essential ingredient is not aboard—and the nearest harbor with a store is a ten-mile beat across the bay. To provision nutritiously and expeditiously, it helps to start with a fairly specific strategy for what you'll be eating when.

It's in this spirit that I offer the following suggested menu plans for three-day and seven-day cruises, plus a complete provisions list for each plan. You can use these lists to plan longer cruises too, so long as there are fairly frequent opportunities to restock en route.

I don't intend for you to follow these plans to the letter—though you can. More likely, you'll want to make substitutions from other recipes in this cookbook, or add favorite recipes of your own, or take advantage of fresh vegetables, fish (or even a restaurant) in the ports you visit. But as you improvise, try to stay within the spirit, at least, of the suggestions I've made here. Keep a generous daily representation of all four food groups in your diet, and when you substitute items, make sure they are of equivalent food value. For example, if you don't like milk or cocoa for breakfast as I suggest on my list, you can drink it at any other meal or swap it for another high-calcium food of equal value, as listed on page

122. The important thing is to be sure you're getting an adequate amount of calcium; how you do it is a matter of personal preference. The other goal to keep in mind as you plan your menus is to use up the most perishable items, such as fresh spinach and strawberries, early in your cruise (for specifics see page 9).

As you can see from my menu plans, my own preference is to prepare certain foods ahead of time and transport them to the boat. If this seems like too much trouble (or takes up too much space in your car), you can cook them aboard almost as easily or else make substitutions. For example, you might want to bring English muffins for breakfast instead of preparing cornbread ahead of time. It *is* helpful to combine some of the dry ingredients for breads, cakes, and pancakes at home because it cuts down on the number of staples you have to lug to the boat. I label these mixtures and store them aboard in large jars or Tupperware containers.

I like to have a generous assortment of spices aboard, not only because they add flavor and variety to food, but because they cut down on the amount of salt used in cooking and eating (for specifics see page 15). For storing spices and herbs on the boat, I've found a method that works well. I bought twenty lightweight, plastic pill bottles (approximately 2 inches high) with childproof screw-on tops from my local pharmacist. I labeled each bottle, then glued one side of Velcro to each bottle cap and the other side to the top of my galley storage cabinet. Believe it or not, those little bottles adhere to the ceiling of the cabinet in the roughest seas, at the same time occupying otherwise wasted storage space.

Finally, you'll note that I've not included any beverages on my menu plans except milk and either orange or grapefruit juice at breakfast (for vitamin C). Other beverages—coffee, tea, alcohol, sodas—are more a matter of personal preference than good nutrition; add those you use to the provisions list.

MENUS FOR FOUR FOR A THREE-DAY CRUISE

*Prepare all or part of recipe ahead of time at home

Day 1

Breakfast
Curried Scrambled Eggs (double recipe, page 42)
Cornbread* (page 32) — *bake entire recipe ahead*
Grapefruit Juice (½ c.)
Skim Milk or Cocoa (1 c.)

Lunch
Lemony Tuna and Beans* (page 53) — *prepare entire recipe ahead*
Lettuce Leaves
Whole Wheat Crackers
Fresh Plums

Dinner
Skillet Chicken Mozzarella (page 78)
Brown Rice Pilaf (page 99)
Broiled Peaches (page 79)
Gingerbread* (page 139) — *bake entire recipe ahead*

Day 2

Breakfast
Banana Bran Pancakes* (page 30) — *combine dry batter ingredients ahead*
Maple Syrup and/or Liquid Corn Oil Margarine (optional)
Low-Fat Sausage Patties* (½ recipe, page 43) — *prepare uncooked patties ahead and freeze*
Orange Juice (½ c.)
Skim Milk or Cocoa (1 c.)

Lunch
Cherry-Nut Chicken Salad in Cantaloupe Bowls* (page 50) — *use canned chicken or cook chicken breasts ahead*
Leftover Cornbread or Whole Wheat Crackers

Dinner
Caesar Salad* (page 115) — *prepare dressing and croutons ahead*
Cheese Fondue (page 111)
Dipping Strawberries (page 123)

Day 3

Breakfast
Whole Wheat and Raisin Griddle Scones* (page 31) — *combine dry batter*
  ingredients ahead
Peanut Butter and/or Jelly
Oatmeal
Orange Juice (½ c.)
Skim Milk or Cocoa (1 c.)

Lunch
Ham and Swiss Cheese Sandwich on Whole Wheat Bread
Fresh Peach

Dinner
Tacos with Seasoned Beef and Cheese* (page 61) — *cook and freeze*
  Seasoned Beef ahead
Chopped Lettuce, Tomatoes, Green Pepper and Onion
Mexican Hot Sauce and Salsa
Bean-Cheese Tortillas (page 61)
Fresh Apple and Orange Slices
Fruit-Granola-Yogurt Sundae with Apricots (page 129)

Provisions To Take On Your Boat
(crew of 4 for 3 days, using above menu plan)

Dairy Foods
Eggs — 8
Cheddar cheese — 4 oz.
Skim milk — 3 qts.
Cocoa mix (optional) — 12 envelopes
Nonfat dry milk powder — 1 envelope for cooking (4 envelopes if also
  used to prepare milk beverage)
Liquid corn oil margarine — 1 small tub
Swiss cheese — 4 oz. sliced
                1 lb. chunk
Part-skim mozzarella cheese — 4 oz. sliced
Fresh parmesan cheese — 2 oz.
Monterey Jack cheese — 1 lb. shredded
Plain low-fat yogurt — 3 c.

Herbs, Spices, and Seasonings
Curry powder
Cayenne pepper
Black pepper

Parsley flakes
Salt
Nutmeg
Cinnamon

Baking Ingredients
Honey
Vanilla extract
Walnuts — ¾ c.
Sugar
Brown sugar

Fruit
Grapefruit juice — 2 c.
Orange juice — 4 c.
Banana — 1 ripe
Cherries or grapes — 2 c.
Apples — 3
Pear — 1
Oranges — 2
Strawberries — 1 qt.
Cantaloupes — 2
Plums — 4
Peaches — 4
Raisins — ½ c.
Canned apricots — 16 oz. can
Canned peach halves — 16 oz. can

Vegetables
Iceberg lettuce — 1 head
Romaine lettuce — 1 large head
Green peppers — 3
Onions — 2 small
Zucchini squash — 2 medium
Tomato — 1 large
Refried beans — 1 can
Bottled spaghetti sauce — 8 oz.

Grains
Oatmeal — 1½ c.
Brown rice — 1½ c.
Whole wheat crackers — 1 box
Taco shells — 10
Tortillas (ready to eat) — 1 box (or unsalted tortilla chips)
Granola — 1 c. (see page 27 if you want to make your own)
French bread — 1 loaf
Whole wheat bread — ½ loaf

Oils and Dressings
Safflower oil
Mayonnaise or mayonnaise-type dressing — 2 small jars

Meats, Fish, and Poultry
Ham, lean — 4 oz.
Chicken breasts, skinned, boned, and split — 2 large whole
Anchovy fillets — 6 (optional)

Miscellaneous
Maple syrup — 1 small bottle
Natural peanut butter — 1 small jar
Sherry — ¼ c.
White wine — 2 c.
Kirschwasser liqueur — 3 oz.
Nonstick spray — 1 can
Raspberry, grape or strawberry jam — 1 small jar
Mexican salsa — 1 jar
Mexican hot sauce — 1 jar

Snack Foods (optional)
Popcorn kernels
Graham crackers
Additional fresh fruit

Ingredients To Have At Home For Food Preparation

Dairy Foods
Eggs
Skim milk

Herbs, Spices, and Seasonings
Salt
Cinnamon
Nutmeg
Ground cloves
Fennel seed
Anise seed
Cayenne pepper
Crushed hot pepper flakes
Lemon pepper seasoning
Garlic Powder
Garlic
Dry mustard
Black pepper
Worcestershire sauce
Chili powder

Cumin
Oregano
Coriander
Hot pepper sauce
Ground ginger

Baking Ingredients
Cornmeal
Whole wheat flour
Wheat germ
Unprocessed bran
All purpose flour
Baking soda
Baking powder
Brown sugar
Sugar
Confectioners' sugar
Blackstrap molasses
Lemon juice

Fruit
Lemons — 3

Vegetables
Celery — 2 stalks
Onions — 1 large and 1 small
Canned cut green beans — 16 oz. can
Canned lima beans — 8 oz. can
Canned garbanzo beans (chick-peas) — 15 oz. can
Canned chopped green chilies — 4 oz. can
Tomato paste — 6 oz. can

Grains
Bread

Oils and Dressings
Safflower oil
Mayonnaise or mayonnaise-type salad dressing
Olive oil

Meat, Fish, and Poultry
Hamburger, lean — 1½ lb.
Chicken breasts — 2 whole
Tuna (water-packed) — 7 oz. can

Miscellaneous
Maple syrup (optional)

MENUS FOR FOUR FOR A SEVEN-DAY CRUISE

*Prepare all or part of recipe ahead of time at home

Day 1

Breakfast
Artichoke-Cheese Scramble (½ recipe, page 41)
Cornbread* (page 32) — bake entire recipe ahead
Orange Juice (½ c.)
Skim Milk or Cocoa (1 c. or serving)

Lunch
Chilled Sesame Lingune* (page 58) — prepare entire recipe ahead
Fruit Salad (1 pear, 1 peach, 4 strawberries and 1 banana)
Carrot-Bran Muffins* (page 34) — bake entire recipe ahead and store leftovers in icebox

Dinner
Lettuce, Tomato, and Cucumber Salad with your favorite dressing
10-Minute Gourmet Chicken (double recipe, page 79)
Brown Rice Pilaf (page 99)
Strawberries Romanoff* (page 124) — prepare strawberries ahead

Day 2

Breakfast
Banana Bran Pancakes* (page 30) — combine dry batter ingredients ahead
Maple Syrup and/or Liquid Corn Oil Margarine (optional)
Low-Fat Sausage Patties* (page 43) — prepare uncooked patties ahead and freeze in 2 batches; use ½ for this meal
Grapefruit Juice (½ c.)
Skim Milk or Cocoa (1 c. or serving)

Lunch
Tuna Salad in Cantaloupe Bowls (page 50)
Whole Wheat Crackers

Dinner
Pressure-Cooked Hamburger and Potato Dinner (page 91)
Carrot-Raisin Salad (page 113)
Steamed Green Beans
Honey-Vanilla Yogurt sprinkled with Granola (recipe times 4, page 128)

Day 3

Breakfast
Granola Split (recipe times 4, page 26)
Orange Juice (½ c.)
Skim Milk or Cocoa (1 c. or serving)

Lunch
Crustless Spinach Pie (page 54)
Fruit Salad (1 peach, 1 pear, 1 banana, and ½ c. grapes)
Whole Wheat Crackers or Pumpernickel Bread

Dinner
Spinach Salad* (page 117) — *prepare dressing ahead*
Cheesy Beans and Rice* (page 104) — *you may want to cook the rice ahead*
Leftover Cornbread
Zucchini Bread* (page 144) — *bake entire recipe ahead*

Day 4

Breakfast
Oatmeal–Whole Wheat Pancakes* (page 29) — *combine dry batter ingredients
    ahead*
Maple Syrup and/or Liquid Corn Oil Margarine
Low-Fat Sausage Patties (page 43) — *use remaining patties*
Grapefruit Juice (½ c.)
Skim Milk or Cocoa (1 c. or serving)

Lunch
Apple-Cheese Toss (page 51)
Whole Wheat Crackers

Dinner
Caesar Salad* (page 115) — *prepare dressing and croutons ahead*
Chicken Diable (page 80) — *follow recipe but use only 3 large, whole chicken
    breasts*
Brown Rice Pilaf (page 99)
Speedy Special Bananas (page 133)

Day 5

Breakfast
Easier and Healthier Eggs Benedict (double recipe, page 40)
Pumpernickel Bread

Orange Juice (½ c.)
Skim Milk or Cocoa (1 c. or serving)

Lunch
Three Bean and Cheese Salad (page 52)
Whole Wheat Crackers
Fresh Plum

Dinner
Baked Ziti with Three Cheeses (page 112)
Broccoli with Lemon-Garlic Sauce (page 118)
Vanilla Pudding (page 131)

Day 6

Breakfast
Leftover Carrot-Bran Muffins
Peanut Butter
Cantaloupe (¼)
Grapefruit Juice (½ c.)
Skim Milk or Cocoa (1 c. or serving)

Lunch
Crabmeat Supreme Sandwich (page 68)
Fresh Peach

Dinner
Lettuce, Tomato, Cucumber, and Green Pepper Salad with any leftover
    dressing
Zucchini Lasagna (page 107)
Baked Potato
Skillet Poppy Seed Cake* (page 141) — *combine dry batter ingredients ahead*

Day 7

Breakfast
Cornmeal Pan Muffins* (page 33) — combine dry batter ingredients
    ahead
Peanut Butter and/or Jam
Oatmeal
Orange Juice (½ c.)
Skim Milk or Cocoa (1 c. or serving)

Lunch
Incredibly Simple Tuna Pie (page 57)
Carrot-Raisin Salad (page 113)
Leftover Bread, Crackers or Muffins

Dinner
Instant Fettucine with Broccoli (page 110)
Broiled Tomatoes
Apple-Yogurt Sundae (page 129)

Depending upon the needs of your crew, you may want to bring additional snacks such as:
Popcorn Kernels
Graham Crackers
Dried Fruits and Nuts
Additional Fresh Fruit
Pumpkin Walnut Cookies* (page 142) — *bake entire recipe ahead*
Tasty Vegetable Dip (page 155) — *with celery and carrot sticks*

Provisions to Take on Your Boat
(crew of 4 for 7 days, using above menu plan)

Dairy Foods
Eggs — 2 dozen
Skim milk — 7 qts.
Cocoa mix — 28 envelopes
Nonfat dry milk powder — 2 envelopes for cooking (9 envelopes if used
  also to prepare milk beverage)
Liquid corn oil margarine — 1 tub
Low-fat cottage cheese — 8 c.
Cheddar cheese — 1¼ lb. shredded
                    3 oz. chunk
Sharp cheddar cheese — 2 oz. shredded
Muenster cheese — 6 oz. chunk
Fresh parmesan cheese — 12 oz.
Part-skim mozzarella cheese — 1 lb. shredded
Plain low-fat yogurt — 8½ c.

Herbs, Spices, and Seasonings
Garlic — 4 cloves
Parsley flakes
Hot pepper seasoning
Worcestershire sauce
Black pepper
Lemon juice

Salt
Basil
Rosemary
Thyme
Sage
Tarragon
Prepared mustard
Curry powder
Dry mustard
Soy sauce
Oregano
Garlic powder
Cinnamon
Nutmeg
Dill weed
Onion powder
Celery seed

Baking Ingredients
Honey — ¾ c.
Vanilla extract
Walnuts — ¾ c.
Slivered almonds — 2 Tbsp.
Pistachio nuts — 3 Tbsp.
Sesame seeds — 2 Tbsp.
Poppy seeds — 1 (2¼ oz.) box
Flour — ¾ c.
Sugar
Brown sugar
Confectioners' sugar
Cornstarch

Fruit
Orange juice — 9 c.
Grapefruit juice — 6 c.
Bananas — 2 ripe and 9 semi-ripe
Cantaloupes — 2 ripe and 1 semi-ripe
Pears — 2
Peaches — 6
Lemons — 4
Grapes — 1 small bunch
Apples — 10
Plums — 4
Limes — 3
Raisins — 2¼ c.
Canned pineapple chunks — 16 oz. can

Vegetables
Green onions or scallions — 1½ bunches
Celery — 1 bunch
Iceberg lettuce — 2 heads
Onions — 3 small, 3 medium, and 1 large
Carrots — 5 lbs.
Zucchini squash — 6 medium
Tomatoes — 6 medium
Cucumbers — 2
Green peppers — 2
Broccoli — 2 large heads
Romaine lettuce — 1 large head
Potatoes — 7 medium and 4 large
Green beans — 1 lb.
Fresh spinach — 1 pkg.
Fresh mushrooms — ½ lb.
Frozen chopped spinach — 10 oz. pkg.
Canned artichoke hearts — 2 (6 oz.) jars
Vegetarian-style beans in tomato sauce — 16 oz. can
Canned cut green beans — 8 oz. can
Canned lima beans — 8½ oz. can
Canned mushroom stems and pieces — 8 oz. can
Tomato sauce — 15 oz. can
Meatless spaghetti sauce — 16 oz. jar
Water chestnuts — 8 oz. can
Canned kidney beans — 15½ oz. can
Canned tomatoes — 16 oz. can
Canned chopped green chilies — 4 oz. can

Grains
Oatmeal — 1⅓ c.
Brown rice — 3½ c.
Bulgur wheat — ⅓ c.
Granola — 2 c.
Ziti macaroni — 8 oz.
Whole wheat fettucine or spaghetti — 8 oz.
Soda crackers — 5
Whole wheat crackers — 2 boxes
Pumpernickel bread — 1 loaf
Whole wheat sandwich buns — 4

Oils and Dressings
Safflower oil
Mayonnaise or mayonnaise-type dressing — 4 small jars
Salad dressing — 1 bottle

Meat, Fish and Poultry
Hamburger, lean — 1½ lbs. (divided into a 1 lb. portion and a ½ lb. portion and frozen)
Chicken breasts, skinned, boned and split — 5 large, whole (freeze 1 pkg. of 3 breasts and leave 2 breasts unfrozen)
Water-packed tuna — 4 (7 oz.) cans
Canned crabmeat — 7½ oz. can
Anchovy fillets — 6 (optional)

Miscellaneous
Maple syrup — 1 bottle
Peanut butter, natural — 1 container
Jam or jelly — 1 small jar
Cognac
Cointreau, Grand Marnier, or Triple Sec liqueur
Nonstick spray — 1 can
Beef bouillon cubes — 2

Snack Foods (optional)
Popcorn kernels
Graham crackers
Additional fresh fruit

Don't forget to bring your pressure cooker if you plan on serving Pressure-Cooked Hamburger and Potato Dinner!

Ingredients to Have at Home for Food Preparation

Dairy Foods
Eggs
Skim milk
Liquid corn oil margarine

Herbs, Spices and Seasonings
Salt
Cinnamon
Nutmeg
Ground cloves
Fennel seed
Anise seed
Cayenne pepper
Crushed hot pepper flakes
Fresh gingerroot
Soy sauce
Wine vinegar

Onion powder
Worcestershire sauce
Catsup
Garlic
Dry mustard
Ground ginger

Baking Ingredients
Cornmeal
Whole wheat flour
Wheat germ
Unprocessed bran
Baking soda
Baking powder
Cream of tartar
White vinegar
Sugar
Brown sugar
Blackstrap molasses
Vanilla extract
Lemon juice
Walnuts

Fruit
Strawberries — 1½ lbs.
Lemons — 2
Raisins — ½ c.

Vegetables
Carrots — 3
Zucchini squash — 1 lb.
Canned pumpkin or squash — 15 oz. can

Grains
Oatmeal
Thin linguine #17 or spaghetti — 1 lb.
Bread

Oils and Dressings
Safflower oil
Sesame or Peanut Oil
Olive oil

Meat, Fish, and Poultry
Hamburger, lean — 1 lb.
Ham, lean — 4 slices

Miscellaneous
Maple syrup
Sesame tahini or peanut butter
Cointreau, Grand Marnier, or Triple Sec liqueur

ADAPTING MENU PLANS FOR OFFSHORE CRUISING

If you are planning a seven-day offshore cruise (such as a voyage to Bermuda), you might want to adapt my menu plans in the following ways:

Breakfasts

1. Skip the pancakes and substitute breads or muffins with peanut butter or cheese.
2. Keep the Eggs Benedict recipe on the menu because you will probably have at least one calm day at sea where you can prepare it.
3. Enjoy the Artichoke-Cheese Scramble before you depart.

Lunches

1. Besides preparing Chilled Sesame Linguine and Carrot-Bran Muffins ahead for your first lunch at sea, I would also bake Crustless Spinach Pie ahead for a lunch later in the week.
2. Incredibly Simple Tuna Pie could be baked on a calm day at sea.
3. I would substitute a lean cold cut sandwich for the Crabmeat Supreme.
4. The rest of the lunch menus are relatively easy to prepare. If you don't feel like making fruit salad, you can eat the fruits individually.
5. Keep an extra supply of crackers and cheese aboard in case there are stormy days when you can't possibly spend any time in the galley.

Dinners

1. Cook, freeze, and portion in foil packs for the oven, Cheesy Beans and Rice, Baked Ziti with Three Cheeses, and Zucchini Lasagna. Use these meals on rough days, simply popping the individual portions into the oven.
2. Substitute a hearty soup such as Lentil Soup for the Chicken Diable because you probably won't want to bother with a recipe that takes an hour to cook. Cook and freeze the soup ahead, and simply reheat it when you need it.
3. Substitute canned or raw vegetables for some of the salads and fresh cooked vegetables on the menus for rough days at sea. (It's nice to

have salads and fresh cooked vegetables, but realistically, you're not going to bother with those at times when you can't stand in the galley.

Desserts

Most of the dessert recipes are very easy to prepare except for Vanilla Pudding and Skillet Poppy Seed Cake, which need to be cooked on the stovetop and should be reserved for calm days.

Snacks

Besides the snack foods already listed, you might want to bake other foods ahead such as Peanut Butter Granola Bars (page 157), Cocoa-Walnut Granola Bars (page 158), or Oatmeal-Banana-Raisin Cookies (page 143). These taste really great on night watches.

Appendix 1

EMERGENCY
SURVIVAL KIT

Most liferafts supply 1 pint of water per person, but do not include any food supplies in the survival pack. Only one liferaft I am aware of supplies some vitamized biscuits and rock candy along with the water—and while these meager, unpalatable rations may provide temporary sustenance, they do little for morale. If you are planning an extended cruise offshore, you would be wise to devote some effort to packing a really adequate survival kit.

WATER

Water is the most essential of all nutrients. You can live for weeks and even months without food but only days without water (generally, 2 to 3 days, depending on the temperature and the amount of energy you expend). You need at least 1 pint of water per person per day for survival, although some survivors have gotten by on as little as ⅓ pint per day for a limited time. The more water you can possibly get aboard the liferaft, the better off you'll be.

When my husband and I sailed to Bermuda, we strapped two 5-gallon jerry cans on deck near the liferaft to be taken aboard in an emergency. (Be sure to leave a few inches or air space at the top of the cans to help them float.) I also kept two 2-quart bottles of water in the emergency food bag.

In addition to bringing water aboard your liferaft, consider other methods of obtaining it:

- Include a solar still.
- Include a desalination apparatus.
- Include a system for collecting rainwater if your liferaft does not already have one.
- Collect dew from the liferaft with a sponge or clothing and suck the moisture from it.

It is also possible to obtain fluids from most marine animals. Cerebrospinal fluid and eyeball fluid contain less salt than human body fluid and are therefore your first choices. Fish juice (except for shark, which is as salty as seawater) and turtle blood are equal in salt content to human body fluid and can be used without detriment. Survival stories abound describing how fish were sucked of their juices to provide desperately needed water.

Whatever you do, don't drink seawater, no matter how much you may desire it. Seawater contains almost four times as much salt as normal body fluid, causing you to become even more dehydrated after drinking it than you were before.

CONSIDERATIONS IN PACKING YOUR SURVIVAL FOOD BAG

Before simply tossing foods into your survival bag, consider these points:

1. Pack foods that are low in sodium, since sodium increases your need for water and promotes dehydration when there is a water shortage.
2. Pack more carbohydrate and fat foods than protein foods because protein foods require more water for metabolism. A diet consisting mostly of protein with few carbohydrates causes dehydration. (If you have ever gone on a high protein, low carbohydrate "fad" diet, you will remember how you lost 2 to 3 pounds of water in the first 2 days.) On days when small amounts of high protein foods are eaten, increase your daily water ration to at least 2 cups of water per person. (If a large amount of protein is eaten, such as a whole fish, 1 quart of water per person per day is recommended.) Remember, the risk of dehydration is much greater than the risk of protein deficiency.
3. Pack foods that are high in water content (and low in sodium) such as fruit juices, canned fruit and unsalted canned vegetables. These foods are heavy to stow, but the most crucial consideration is that they supply vitally needed water.

FOOD SUGGESTIONS FOR YOUR SURVIVAL FOOD BAG

Pack as many of the following foods as your smallest crew member can comfortably lift in a large bag (we used our nylon jib bag). Choose more high-carbohydrate foods than high-protein foods, and favor the fruit-vegetable group because of its high water content. Remember to keep the survival bag next to the companionway at all times so that it is easy to grab in an emergency.

Milk Group (high in protein and carbohydrates):
1-qt. envelopes of nonfat dry milk (stored in a plastic zip-sealed bag)
Canned nutritional milk beverages

Meat Group (high in protein and fat):
Unsalted canned fish, poultry, or meat
Unsalted peanut butter
Unsalted nuts

Fruit-Vegetable Group (high in carbohydrates and water):
Small cans or boxes of orange or grapefruit juice (for vitamin C)
Small cans or boxes of other juices of your choice (avoid tomato or vegetable juice unless it is unsalted)
Canned fruit (citrus sections, peaches, apricots, and purple plums are the most nutritious)
Unsalted canned vegetables (tomatoes, carrots, spinach, turnip greens, asparagus, peas, potatoes, pumpkin, sweet potatoes, and green and wax beans are the most nutritious)
Dried fruit such as apricots, peaches, prunes, raisins, dates, and figs (low in water content)

Grain Group (high in carbohydrates):
Unsalted crackers
Graham crackers
Unsalted granola

Also include:
2 2-qt. containers of water (I use old soda bottles filled to 2 inches from the top and sealed with electrical tape)
Multiple vitamin and mineral tablets (to provide 100% of the RDA)

Make sure that all noncanned or bottled items are sealed in airtight containers or zip-sealed bags. If you have to use your liferaft, it will most likely get very wet inside, particularly when boarding in heavy seas.

OTHER ESSENTIAL ITEMS TO INCLUDE IN THE FOOD BAG

2 can openers
Drinking vessel
2 knives (well wrapped to prevent accidental puncturing of the liferaft)
zip-sealed plastic bags
sponges to collect dew
fishing tackle

For advice on additional non-food-related survival items such as medical supplies, sun signalling mirror, flares, EPIRB (Emergency Position Indication Radio Beacon), charts, whistle, space blanket, dry clothing, etc., consult the following excellent reference books:

Cohen, Michael Martin. Dr. Cohen's Healthy Sailor Book. Camden: International Marine Publishing Company, 1983.
Lee, E.C.B., and Kenneth Lee. Safety and Survival at Sea. New York: Norton, 1971.

RECOMMENDED READING LIST

Brody, Jane. Jane Brody's Nutrition Book. New York: Bantam Books, 1981. An excellent book for enjoyable reading on nutrition and healthful eating.

Clark, Nancy. The Athlete's Kitchen—A Nutrition Guide and Cookbook. Boston: CBI Publishing Company, 1981. Although this book is intended for athletes, it is chock-full of interesting nutrition information. Many of the recipes in this book are quick and easy and would be usable on a sailboat.

Lappé, Frances Moore. Diet for a Small Planet. Rev. ed., New York: Ballantine Books, 1982. A detailed reference for information on protein complementation.

Robertson, Laurel, Carol Flinders, and Bronwen Godfrey. Laurel's Kitchen—A Handbook for Vegetarian Cookery and Nutrition. Berkeley: Nilgeri Press, 1976. An easy-to-read reference and cookbook on vegetarianism and nutrition in general.

Appendix 2

FAT GRAMS

- Light mayonnaise refers to varieties with 50% less fat.
- You may wish to substitute low-fat cheese (4–5 grams fat per oz.) for regular cheese (8–9 grams fat per oz.) to substantially lower the fat content of some recipes.

Recipe	Fat Grams per Serving (rounded off to the nearest gram)
10-Minute Gourmet Chicken	8
Apple Crisp	7
Apple-Cheddar Broil	10
Apple-Cheese Toss	27 with mayonnaise 17 with light mayonnaise
Apple-Yogurt Sundae	less than 1
Artichoke-Cheese Scramble	26
Babaganouj	24 per entire recipe
Baked Custard	2

(continued on next page)

Recipe	Fat Grams per Serving (rounded off to the nearest gram)
Baked Ziti with Three Cheeses	13
Banana Bran Pancakes	13
Banana Cake	14
Barley with Dill	4
Beau Monde Dip	6 with mayonnaise 2 with light mayonnaise
Blueberry or Other Fruit Crisp	13
Broiled Peaches	0
Brown Rice Pilaf	3
Browned Oats	9
Butterscotch Pudding	6
Cabbage-Cheddar Chowder	16 with beef 9 without beef
Caesar Salad	13
Canned Corned Beef and Cheese Sandwiches	15
Carrot-Bran Muffins	3
Carrot-Orange Cake	10
Carrot-Raisin Salad	15 with mayonnaise 5 with light mayonnaise less than 1 with yogurt
Carrot-Raisin Salad with Cheese	28 with mayonnaise 19 with light mayonnaise 14 with yogurt

(continued on next page)

Recipe	Fat Grams per Serving (rounded off to the nearest gram)
Cheese Fondue	21
Cheese-Carrot Spread	3 with mayonnaise 2 with light mayonnaise
Cheesy Beans and Rice	10
Cherry-Nut Chicken Salad	29 with mayonnaise 15 with light mayonnaise 7 with yogurt
Chicken Diable	9 following recipe 13 with double sauce
Chicken Dijon	6
Chicken Marsala	8
Chili Corn Chowder	5
Chili Dip	less than 1
Chilled Sesame Linguine	9
Chocolate Cake with Chocolate Sauce	4
Chocolate Pudding	2
Cinnamon-Glazed Carrots	7 with walnuts 3 without walnuts
Cocoa-Walnut Granola Bars	4
Cornbread	3
Cornmeal Pan Muffins	1
Crabmeat Supreme Sandwiches	17 with mayonnaise 10 with light mayonnaise
Creamed Cabbage and Walnut Casserole	28

(continued on next page)

Recipe	Fat Grams per Serving (rounded off to the nearest gram)
Creamy Cucumbers	less than 1
Crustless Spinach Pie	16
Curried Scrambled Eggs	17
Dipping Strawberries	less than 1 gram
Easier and Healthier Eggs Benedict	19 with mayonnaise 12 with light mayonnaise
Eggplant-Artichoke Parmesan Casserole	18
English Muffin Pizzas	7
Fruit-Granola-Yogurt Sundae	6
Gingerbread	7
Granola	5
Granola Split	6
Guacamole	3
Ham and Pineapple Sandwiches	21
Herbed Crunch	12
Hibachi Dessert Kabobs	7
Hibachi Peanut Chicken or Pork Kabobs	7 with chicken 11 with pork
Homemade Cocoa Mix	less than 1
Honey-Vanilla Yogurt	less than 1
Hummus	31 per entire recipe

(continued on next page)

Recipe	Fat Grams per Serving (rounded off to the nearest gram)
Incredibly Simple Tuna Pie	22 with mayonnaise 13 with light mayonnaise 8 with yogurt
Instant Dip	less than 1
Instant Fettucine	12
Instant Fettucine with Broccoli	12
Kasha	3
Layered Tossed Salad	30 with regular mayonnaise-type salad dressing 22 with light mayonnaise-type salad dressing
Lemon-Garlic Sauce for Vegetables	7 with regular mayonnaise 3 with light mayonnaise
Lemony Tuna and Beans	17 with mayonnaise 8 with light mayonnaise 2 with yogurt
Lentil Soup	less than 1
Low-Fat "Sausage" Patties	6
Meringue Bowls with Fresh Fruit	less than 1 (not including whipped cream or yogurt)
Mexican Munchies	12
Molasses Cakes	5
Nachos	21 with regular tortilla chips 13 with low fat baked tortilla chips
No-Fat French Fries	0
Nonfat Dry Milk Drinks	less than 1

(continued on next page)

Recipe	Fat Grams per Serving (rounded off to the nearest gram)
Nutty Egg and Green Bean Sandwiches	24 with mayonnaise 20 with light mayonnaise
Nutty Popcorn Balls	7
Oat Bran Cereal	3
Oatmeal-Banana-Raisin Cookies	3
Oatmeal-Oat Bran Coffee Cake	13
Oatmeal-Oat Bran Muffins	10
Oatmeal-Walnut Cake	16
Oatmeal-Whole Wheat Pancakes	5
One-Skillet Beef-Noodle Medley	20
Open-Faced Mozzarella and Peppers	6
Open-Faced Mushroom and Cheddar Cheese Sandwiches	13
Open-Faced Reubens	16
Parmesan Popcorn	9
Pasta Primavera	17
Peaches with Honey-Lime Yogurt	less than 1
Peanut Butter Candies	3
Peanut Butter-Cottage Cheese-Raisin Sandwiches	13
Peanut Butter-Granola Bars	13
Picadillo	26
Pineapple Flambe'	0

(continued on next page)

Recipe	Fat Grams per Serving (rounded off to the nearest gram)
Poor Man's Lobster	13
Potato Crisps	0
Pressure-Cooked Hamburger and Potato Dinner	13
Pressure-Cooked Whole Wheat Bread	3
Pumpkin Pie	7 with crust 0 without crust
Pumpkin-Walnut Cookies	3
Quick Cocoa-Oatmeal Chewies	3
Quick Fish Chowder	3
Salmon Loaf with Dill Sauce	8
Skillet Chicken Mozzarella	10
Skillet Poppy Seed Cake	6
Soybean Casserole	25
Speedy Special Bananas	2
Spiced Roast Beef Spread Sandwiches	13
Spinach Pie with Yogurt	7 without crust 17 with crust
Spinach Salad with Cheese	19 with cheese (not including dressing) 3 without cheese (not including dressing) 4 per 1 Tbsp. dressing
Steaks Au Poivre Pavillon	16
Stir-Fried Chicken with Nuts	15

(continued on next page)

Recipe	Fat Grams per Serving (rounded off to the nearest gram)
Stirred Custard	3
Strawberries Romanoff	2 with nuts less than 1 without nuts
Summer Pasta Salad	27
Summer Squash and Cheese Quiche	15
Tabouli	10
Tahini-Yogurt-Lemon Sauce	3
Tamale Pie with or without Cheese	12 with cheese 3 without cheese
Tasty Vegetable Dip	6 with mayonnaise 2 with light mayonnaise
Three Bean and Cheese Salad	8
Tuna Salad in Cantaloupe Bowls	18 with mayonnaise 9 with light mayonnaise 4 with yogurt
Vanilla Pudding	2
Vegetarian Pocket Sandwiches	8
Whole Wheat and Raisin Griddle Scones	7
Whole Wheat Irish Soda Bread	1
Whole Wheat Irish Soda Bread with Wheat Sprouts	1
Whole Wheat Pancakes with Blueberry Sauce	6
Whole Wheat Pie Crust	10
Whole Wheat Pizza	14

(continued on next page)

Recipe	Fat Grams per Serving (rounded off to the nearest gram)
Whole Wheat Sesame Cereal	6
Wonderful Chicken Curry	11
Zucchini Bread	3
Zucchini Lasagna	13

Appendix 3

THE FOOD
GUIDE PYRAMID

Since this book was written in 1986, The Basic Four Food Guide has been replaced by The Food Guide Pyramid. Nutrition experts felt that the Basic Four put equal emphasis on all four groups, whereas it is now felt that we should be eating much more from the Fruit, Vegetable, and Bread groups, adequate amounts from the Milk Group, and for most Americans, much less from the Meat Group.

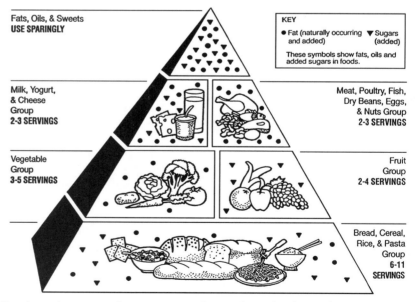

Serving sizes are the same as those described in The Four Food Groups, pages 6–12.

Appendix 4

ANTIOXIDANTS AND PHYTOCHEMICALS

Another major reason to eat more from the Vegetable, Fruit, and Bread Groups is that many of the foods in these groups contain substances (antioxidants and phytochemicals) that may protect us against some forms of cancer, aging, and other chronic illnesses such as heart disease. Here is a list of the most powerful of these health-promoting foods:

Almonds
Apricots
Broccoli
Brussels sprouts
Cabbage
Cantaloupe
Carrots
Carrot juice
Cauliflower
Filberts
Grapefruit
Greens

Guava
Hazelnuts
Kale
Kiwi fruit
Mango
Okra
Oranges
Papaya
Peppers
Pumpkin
Romaine

Spinach
Strawberries
Sunflower oil
Sunflower seeds
Sweet potato
Tangerines
Tomato
Watermelon
Wheat germ
Whole grains
Winter squash

INDEX

ABOUT
THE AUTHOR

Joan Betterley, a Registered Dietitian, earned her B.S. in Nutrition from Pennsylvania State University. As the creator and Director of the Nutrition Department at the Fallon Clinic in Worcester, Massachusetts, she developed therapeutic diets for patients and taught nutrition classes. Previously, she was a Clinical Dietitian at two Massachusetts hospitals: Nashoba Community and St. Vincent. She has written nutritional guides, and contributed to *The Athlete's Kitchen* and *Nancy Clark's Sports Nutrition Guidebook*.

Joan currently lives in Massachusetts, where she and her husband, Rick, are raising two children. Their boat, *Quiet Harbor* is moored in Friendship, Maine. The Betterleys sailed the Maine coast and to Bermuda and back while Joan experimented with many tasty, healthy recipes.